Coffee with God and Joy in the Spring Mornings

90 Sips of Strong Grace, Bold Faith, and Endless Mercy

Debb Joy

DEEP WATERS BOOKS

Coffee with God and Joy in the Spring Mornings: 90 Sips of Strong Grace, Bold Faith, and Endless Mercy

Copyright © 2026 Debb Joy

Published by Deep Waters Books, P.O. Box 692301, Orlando, FL 32869

First Printing 2026

Printed in the United States of America

Identifiers: 978-1-956520-21-7 (Hardcover) | 978-1-956520-44-6 (paperback) | 2026905184 LCCN

Publisher's Cataloging-in-Publication data

Names: Joy, Debb, author.

Title: Coffee with God and joy in the spring mornings: 90 sips of strong grace, bold faith, and endless mercy / Debb Joy

Description: Orlando, FL: Deep Waters Books, 2025.

Identifiers: ISBN: 978-1-956520-21-7 (hardcover) | 978-1-956520-44-6 (paperback) | 2026905184 LCCN

Subjects: LCSH Christian women--Prayers and devotions. | Christian life. | Bible--Study and teaching. | Faith. | Suffering--Religious aspects--Christianity. | Bereavement--Religious aspects--Christianity. | Grief--Religious aspects-- Christianity. | Consolation. | Devotional calendars. | Meditations. | BISAC RELIGION / Devotional | RELIGION / Christian Life / Personal Growth | RELIGION / Christian Life / Death, Grief, Bereavement | RELIGION / Christian Life / Women's Issues Classification: LCC BV4844 .C544 2019 | DDC 242/.643—dc23

Endorsements

Genuine, authentic, and Spirit-filled encouragement from one of West Texas's finest ladies. Debbie Joy writes with a heartfelt desire to see people draw closer to our Lord and Savior, Jesus Christ.

~ Daniel Thiebaud, Pastor, Brushy Top Cowboy Church, Eldorado, Texas

I have known Debbie Joy for fifteen years, and during that time, her testimony has remained consistent in her daily walk with God. She has touched the lives of so many people with her Christian devotionals.

~ Reneé Butts, Retired HR Specialist, Concho Valley Electric Co-op, Mertzon, Texas

Morning and coffee, they go together like—well, like morning and coffee. A time to reflect and maybe even relax before the day begins. A time to stop and think and plan. A time to be thankful for being given another morning. A time to be still.

During those quiet moments in the morning over a cup of coffee, or on a long straight stretch of highway or horseback, or wherever you make time to be still. God will speak to you in whatever way you hear Him.

Debb Joy has been gifted with the ability to be still and listen to God. She has also been called to put in writing what she learns during these times and share it with the rest of us. So, I encourage you to enjoy these writings and let them be the "coffee" in your mornings. Then be still and let God speak through her words first and then through your thoughts as you go through the rest of the day.

May you find joy in the morning.

May you be inspired to be the word of encouragement for someone else.

Thank you, Debb. Keep listening and keep writing.

~ Doug Tolleson, PhD of Rangeland, Associate Professor, Ecology and Management, Sonora, Texas

During a recent time of great stress, I have been blessed to discover the words Debb Joy writes during her quiet time each morning.

Those words have strengthened, uplifted, and encouraged me. Instead of ego, I have seen a refreshing humility. Even more crucially, her words have always pointed with bedrock faith to the God of Debb's hope. Despite the heartbreak of unspeakable grief and the bruises of everyday life, Debb's faith and joy shine through in each simple, concise, and thoughtful piece of writing.

~ Martha Sue Oliver, wife, mother, grandmother, and beloved child of the King, San Angelo, Texas

I feel so grateful and fortunate to know Debb Joy. She has been an inspiration on many levels for a long time. Her daily writings have brought depth of clarity, peace, security, and encouragement. Her content is scripturally accurate, relevant, understandable, and *applicable in helping us to grow closer to the Lord Jesus and thereby live more and more as He wants. We are progressively transformed into His image by the power of the Indwelling Holy Spirit. Thank you, Debb!*

~ Steve Sessom, Retired DDS, adult Sunday school teacher, small group Bible study leader, preacher as needed, and long-term Bible student

No one likes to be "in charge" as much as I do!

"My way or the highway" was always one of the guiding principles of my life—until I started coffee with God and Debb Joy each morning. I am now "letting go of the illusion of control and embracing the freedom of trusting in his provision."

Debb is a role model and mentor to the young ladies in her church's music ministry. Through her example, she is making a huge difference in their lives. Working with students, I have learned that they may listen to what you say, but you can be sure they are watching what you do. Debb not only talks the talk, but she walks the walk with the Lord every day. I am fortunate to know and love her and experience the grace of God through her efforts!

~ Nancy Lester, Retired County Extension Agent, Eldorado, Texas

Debb Joy is the real deal. I've seen her in the deepest of grief and the highest of joys, and she continues to be a faith-filled, encouraging disciple of Jesus. Once her pastor—I'm now her student. She draws me closer to the Savior with every devotional. No fluff—straight to the heart.

Get ready for God to work on you because the Spirit speaks through Debb Joy!

~ Reverend Leo Wideman, Kerrville, TX

A "happy-happy" faux-Christian—Debb Joy is NOT! Her faith is real, refined, and tempered in the crucible of a life filled with more than her share of loss, challenges, and reversals. Yet, there she remains—a light that brings us back from the abyss to God's unfathomable love and grace.

~ Harold Skaggs Jr., MD, Elder, Leader of Men in the Word Bible Study, Austin, TX

Debb Joy is a force of nature. I have known her all of my life, and two of her traits have stood out consistently in all circumstances: her love for the Lord and her love of life and people. She stands with "one foot raised," ready to respond to the Lord's call with joy and passion wherever she is led. Debb is a treasure and a gift!

~ Jan Morrow Skaggs, Elder, Teacher of Lamplighters Bible Study, Austin, TX

Coffee with God starts daily by genuinely delighting in the Lord's presence. Debb Joy is a true servant who has faithfully used her gifts to bring him glory and further the kingdom.

~ Savannah Chambers, Office Manager, First Baptist Church Sonora, Sonora, TX

It would be hard to find a better person than Debb Joy to guide us into a deeper relationship with the Lord. Through her personal experiences, wisdom, and humor, we are drawn into the wisdom of her daily devotionals, creating a desire for more of the Lord's presence in our lives.

~ Carolyn Price, Director of Children's Choir, First Presbyterian Church, Midland, TX

To those who seek to love God big and run daily after our Lord, give them a copy of this devotional. Debb's devotion to Jesus, along with her personal life, struggles, and victories, gives her a unique, grace-filled perspective on faith, hope, and how to walk with Jesus.

Debb, my sister in Christ, mentor, and dear friend, is a great encourager in the faith. She has inspired me to grow spiritually, love others, and find joy in the Lord's presence. She walks through the wilderness with you and kneels fervently in daily prayer in her real prayer closet. Join her in the prayer closet and find peace, hope, and joy in Jesus.

~ Kristy D. Edwards, MD, CWS-P, FAAFP, Primary Care and Rural Medicine, School of Medicine, Texas A&M University

I am blessed to know Debb as a fellow prayer warrior, Sunday school teacher, mentor to many, fireball of a friend, servant, and sister in Christ. I know firsthand that her heart is always seeking, listening, and obeying the Lord. Her last name, Joy, also perfectly describes her personality: sharing joy with others.

For the last several years, I have had the privilege of waking up each morning to a text message of Scripture and a devotional message from Debb. These started several years ago when she knew I needed them the most. I am one of many who have the privilege to receive these daily encouragements. She shares meaningful lessons that are sincere, spirit-led, sometimes humorous and serious, but ALWAYS applicable.

Now, with this wonderful book, you can share in Debb's "Joy" with the most heartfelt of her daily devotions. Spend time with the Lord each day reading each message, and you, too, will learn more about God's Word, Debb's heart, and her mission to share his Word with others.

~ Shelly Shannon, Retired Public School Teacher, Sonora ISD, Sonora, TX

Debb is inarguably the most joyful person I have ever met. Her ability to encourage people by using the Word of God is unparalleled. I consider myself blessed to be her pastor and see her faith live out daily.

~ Matt Killough, Senior Pastor, First Baptist Church, Sonora, TX

Contents

Dedication

*I lovingly dedicate this book
to the love of my life,
my husband Kerry,
who makes my heart skip a beat
and leap for joy.*

*Thank you all for reminding me daily,
that having somewhere to go is home;
having someone to love is family;
and to have both is a blessing.*

You are my blessing in this life.

In loving memory of my
Carmen Joy (1977–2011)

From the Heart

In February of 1977, I gave birth to our firstborn, a beautiful auburn-haired baby girl, Carmen Joy. Like any newlywed couple, my husband and I were ecstatic and envisioned the beginnings of our fairy tale—a happily married couple, the addition of more babies, a new puppy, and a small house that we called home.

Within eight months of our precious infant's birth, Carmen was diagnosed with cystic fibrosis. Devastation set in for both my husband and me. I drew from the same fount of strength I gulped from in my youth.

When I was a child, my mother had taught me the art of journaling. Throughout my high school years, I spent hours recording my most intimate thoughts concerning life's hard knocks, heartbreaks, cheerleader tryouts, boyfriends, jealousy, envious friends, and disappointments. Now, watching my young baby struggle, I turned my thoughts into written prayers. The years of practice spent recording the drama of high school now became my lifeline. Little did I know as I recorded my deepest pain, these words and times with my eternal Father would get me *through the darkest days of my adult life. The joy of the Lord came every morning as I had my coffee with God.*

Thirty-four years later, in 2011, our darling Carmen returned to our eternal Father. Years later, these four-seasonal devotionals, "Coffee with God: Joy in the Mornings: 90 Sips of Strong Grace, Bold Faith, and Endless Mercy," are a reality.

I'm indebted to all those who contributed their experiences, joys, sorrows, moments of doubt, stories of unshakeable faith, and testimonies. I pored over Sarah Young devotionals, books from the late Billy Graham and many others, including Max Lucado, and in them I found peace in God. I am so grateful for their obedience in writing down their faith-filled exhortations. I know I couldn't have gone through the fires of purification without their sweet words of encouragement.

To my amazing husband, my younger and extraordinary daughter, Madolyn Marie, and the many others who helped carry me through such sadness and darkness, I am so thankful for your love, support, and care. My amazing daughter, Madolyn, lovingly created each of these beautiful illustrations at the start of each month for all four 90-day devotionals.

I now believe more firmly than ever in the power of prayer. Most importantly, I am eternally grateful to God for the miraculous outpouring of grace, love, and faith he has lavished on our family and me.

From those whose paths we will probably never cross again, such as the doctors, nurses, and staff of Houston Methodist Hospital, to the people closest to me, please know that your unwavering faith and prayers have forged a deeper bond with my Savior that I never thought possible. My utmost appreciation to the special group that made this book come to fruition, especially Deep Waters Books, my publisher; my prayer warrior, and friend, Kim M. Clark; and Krista Murr, another devout prayer soldier and treasured friend, who, without her, these devotionals would have never made it into the right hands.

Of course, my most loving support team will forever be my family. My husband, Kerry, is my fiercest ally and has always allowed me to immerse myself in emotional experiences. My daughter, Madolyn, her husband, and my two handsome grandsons have been a constant and faithful source of strength in my daily life. I'm personally honored to have this book's illustrations brought to you, the reader, from my grandson and his gifted mother.

I pray Carmen's favorite verse comforts you and your family as it has us for so many years: "'For I know the plans I have for you,' declares the LORD, 'plans to prosper you and not to harm you, plans to give you hope and a future'" (Jeremiah 29:11 NIV).

Love, joy, and peace,

Debb Joy

Spring

Spring is when we get our much-needed rainfall.
The grass is so green and smells so alive.
Baby lambs, fawns, and calves abound
as mommas are having twins and triplets.

This is the renewal season.

The time of new life.

March

March 1
NO FEAR!

For God has not given us a spirit of fear and timidity,
but of power, love, and self-discipline.
~ 2 Timothy 1:7

Fear can cause us to stop dead in our tracks and question what our Father has told us to do. I can't tell you how many times I question God, especially when he is telling me to do something that I don't want to do. For me, I allow the spirit of fear to enter into my life because I don't know what lies ahead of me and I forget that God is already there.

Then, after I pray, I remind myself that I should only fear God and nothing else, as "it is a terrible thing to fall into the hands of the living God" (Hebrews 10:31).

Paul had to encourage his protégé, Timothy, a younger, timid man and probably not physically strong, to rebuke the spirit of fear and embrace God's gift of power, love, and self-discipline. Timothy knew of Paul's frequent trials, and thinking he might suffer those same persecutions, he allowed fear to enter his thoughts.

Thankfully, we can draw on the power of the Holy Spirit to enable us to see things as God sees them. There is no reason to live in fear when we have the mighty presence of the Spirit of God within us.

God, free me from any fears
and open my eyes to your love and protection.
Increase the work of the Holy Spirit in me
of love, power, and self-discipline.
Help me remember,
we are told repeatedly in the Bible,
"Fear not!"

March 2

God's Perfect Design for Your Life

For everything there is a season,
a time for every activity under heaven.
~ Ecclesiastes 3:1

Just as God planned seasons in nature, he prearranged the seasons in our lives as well. We have experienced several blistering cold days this spring, which is unusual for us. Because we are accustomed to milder winters and early springs in Texas, everyone seemed to need a break from the cold, damp, gray skies. I know I was ready for some sunshine and warmth.

Winter brings an end to a particular period in our lives. This could be a hardship or a time of growth, but with God, we remain hopeful, knowing spring is around the corner. It is important that we remember this time is only for a season and it will pass.

In God's perfect design, he provides us with a variety of spiritual seasons. Times of fruitfulness and activity; times for quiet and rest;

times to trust him when he asks us to remain faithful doing the same work, day after day; and times of excitement for new beginnings.

By God's grace, we will overcome the cold winters of heartache, grief, and healing, for without winter, we would never get to experience spring.

The different seasons in our lives work together to fulfill God's perfect plan for us. Take a moment to gaze upward and bask in the radiance of his divine presence.

Dear God, help me trust you
through each season of my life—
even the dark days of winter.

March 3
Help me, Lord, I'm Drowning!

I long, yes,
I faint with longing to enter the courts of the LORD.
With my whole being, body and soul,
I will shout joyfully to the living God.
~ Psalm 84:2

Sometimes, life gets in the way and my quiet time with God wanes. I am irritable and short-tempered with those I am surrounded by and love the most. When I confessed my sin, the Holy Spirit convicted me that my behavior was a direct result of missing the most important thing in my life—time with my Father.

Not spending time with God is like being underwater for too long, as the pressure intensifies and the minutes tick away. Your lungs start to burn as your mind realizes drowning is a possibility. As your body's reflex to live takes over, you desperately try to reach the surface. Rushing to do so becomes the top priority. Mercifully, you break the water surface and gasp for a breath of fresh air.

Just like air, our bodies, souls, and minds need time to recharge with our Maker. Our heart craves his peace and comfort. It is then that we realize how desperately we need God even more than the air we breathe. Being filled with his Spirit becomes more important than anything else. God's desire for us is to find complete satisfaction in him alone. When I gulp in his presence, I'm reminded of how loving and dear my Father is to me.

Dear God, give me a renewed hunger for you.
Become my sustenance and nourishment.
I now realize I need you more than the air I breathe.
I joyfully shout your praises.

March 4
A Classic Example of One Who Endured

Therefore, since we are surrounded by such a huge crowd
of witnesses to the life of faith,
let us strip off every weight that slows us down,
especially the sin that so easily trips us up.
And let us run with endurance
the race God has set before us.
~ Hebrews 12:1

As a sprinter in high school, I found preparing and competing for my races to be sheer agony. In the New Testament, the authors wrote about running, as we are "running the race set before [us]" (2 Timothy 4:7). Interestingly enough, the Greek word for *contest* is *agōn*, from which we get the word *agony*. I would agree.

The Christian race is not a slow, easy jog but rather a demanding and grueling marathon. Long-distance running takes massive effort and training to finish strong. Over the years, I've seen a few saints who have struggled toward the end of their race. In their prime, they were amazing contenders and kept a strong pace. Then weariness, the cares of life, loss, or illness set in, causing them to stumble and fall.

Such is the life of a Christian. I'd be willing to bet we've all experienced spiritual weariness at one time or another. Church attendance decreases, we drop out of fellowship, and our quiet times with God become as nonexistent as our prayer life as we become spiritually dehydrated. Tithing ceases and our offerings are only what is left over after our bills are paid at the end of the month. We are just going through the motions. Our hearts are far from God.

Jesus's best work was his final work. He could have given up, thrown in the towel, and gone home. But he didn't. What will you do? Will you run the entire race before you?

Faithful Father,
when I grow faint and weary,
carry me across the finish line.

March 5

Through the Storm of Judgment

Yes, this anguish was good for me,
for you have rescued me from death
and forgiven all my sins.
~ Isaiah 38:17

All of my life, I never thought of myself as prideful until the Holy Spirit revealed that the root of my desire for perfection is—are you ready for this?—pride. Some of us are so blind to this sin in our lives as we work, push, and strive so we can prove that *I am worthy . . . I am the best . . . I deserve honors . . . and look at me!*

Pride is the source of these dead-end proclamations that oppose God. They mean nothing in the kingdom of heaven! Those truths don't make me feel all warm and fuzzy inside. Now I see how much pride grieves the Holy Spirit.

We will never truly comprehend the extent of God's love for Christ at the cross until we hear the crowd screaming, "Crucify!

Crucify!" Our Savior has already taken the judgment that you and I deserve. Jesus's complete work on the cross redeemed us.

As believers in Jesus Christ, we have already come through the storm of judgment and are victorious. Don't allow the enemy to bind you anymore to your past—to what you've done, poor decisions you made, or any fears, anger, or regrets. Realize, once and for all, that sin's penalty for our sins has already been paid, completely and fully by Christ.

God, I humbly ask you, our righteous Judge,
to replace my foolish pride with a spirit of humility
and praise for your Son's complete work
on the cross for me.
Thank you for forgiving all my sins.

March 6
What Difference Does It Make?

The people said to Joshua,
"We will serve the Lord our God.
We will obey him alone."
~ Joshua 24:24

There is a story about a wealthy father who refused to get his son a bicycle because the boy's report card showed disgracefully low grades, the yard was not raked, and the dishwasher had not been unloaded. The father wasn't being cruel or stingy; he simply knew his son needed to learn responsibility and live up to his potential.

In my late sixties, I am convicted. I, too, struggle with doing what needs to be done first. I want to do fun things first. I know that I am absolutely saved by his grace, but I am also called to be a disciple of Christ, and my actions reflect my Savior. I need to follow Christ and obey God's will, regardless of my age. The Bible warns, "If you do not obey the LORD, and if you rebel against his commands, his hand will be against you" (1 Samuel 12:15 NIV).

Do you want to unleash the power of prayer in your life?

Choose to obey God. Become immersed in his truths through his Word. Pray for God to identify any areas of disobedience that might be impeding your endeavors. Reflect on the impact of your actions and ask yourself, "Will it make an eternal difference?" for true significance lies in the eternal.

Dear God, help me always put you first.
Give me the strength to obey you through your Word.
Allow me to always remember that my obedience
does make a difference to you and
others who are watching me
as one of your children.

March 7

An Encounter with God

Now get up and stand on your feet.
I have appeared to you to appoint you as a servant
and as a witness of what you have seen
and will see of me.
~ Acts 26:16

Have you ever had an encounter with God? I believe all of us do in one form or another. This could be a gentle nudge to bless someone with a meal, gift, or phone call. Or maybe something more impactful like a vivid dream about Jesus beckoning us to come to him. Or even a miraculous healing or deliverance.

Regardless of the type of our interaction, the good news is that God was working in our lives long before we even began working with him. The Lord knew you before time began, and he already decreed what he wanted to do with your life (see Jeremiah 1:5; Psalm 139:13).

God loves you enough to allow his only Son to be sacrificed for you so he can have sweet communion with you. And then for his Holy Spirit to be poured into you to give you the wisdom you need every day. We are not God's robots that he programs each day with a daily devotional in an attempt to simply increase our biblical knowledge.

God desires us to walk humbly with him. Sometimes we get a glimpse of what he is doing. And we get to join him in the work he is doing.

Are you prepared to have an encounter with God today?

Dear faithful God, prepare me for the day ahead.
Make me ready and willing to go
wherever you want me to go,
say whatever you want me to say,
and be who you want me to be.
Give me attentive ears to hear your guidance.

March 8

How Well Do You Know Judas?

You, therefore, have no excuse,
you who pass judgment on someone else,
for at whatever point you judge another,
you are condemning yourself,
because you who pass judgment do the same things.
~ Romans 2:1

I've wondered at times what kind of man this Judas was. How did he look? What were his actions? Who were his friends?

Some question his relationship with the Master. Judas had heard Christ speak and saw him perform miracles, but did he really know Jesus as Lord? Perhaps Judas had religion but no relationship. I wonder if the devil worked his way around the disciples, searching for a special kind of man to betray our Lord? Was Judas selected because he saw Jesus but did not know him?

Satan's best tools of destruction are not from outside the fellowship of Christians; rather, they are from *within* the body of believers. The church will never die from the immorality in Hollywood or the corruption in Washington. Some believe it will perish from corrosion within caused by those who bear the name of Jesus but have never met him.

That was me. Years ago, I had religion but no personal relationship with Jesus Christ as my Lord and Savior. I was like Judas, who bore the cloak of religion but never knew the heart of Christ. Mercifully, God saved me and turned my heart of stone into one of flesh.

Do you have religion or Jesus in your heart?

*Dear God, change my heart from one of stone
to one of flesh. Ignite my personal relationship with you.
Convict me when I judge others.
Instill in me a humble heart of compassion.
Give me guidance and strength
to follow only in your path.*

March 9
Ordinary People Facing Mount Everest

"What do you mean, 'If I can'?"
Jesus asked. "Anything is possible if a person believes."
The father instantly cried out,
"I do believe, but help me overcome my unbelief!"
~ Mark 9:23–24

What is your most desperate prayer? Is a rebellious child breaking your heart? Is it the threat of losing a loved one to cancer? The need to pay tomorrow's bills with no funds in the bank?

When our beloved Carmen went home to be with the Lord, I struggled with God's answer to our prayers for her healing. I never liked hearing no. When it came to my daughter, I didn't ever think my heart would heal. Those were dark days during my faith walk.

During times of testing, we may go days or weeks without consistent prayer, but then something happens. A sermon or a Christian song pierces the deep grief in our heart and lifts our spirit to new heights. But then another tragedy suddenly strikes, and something once again leads us to submerge ourselves in prayer and then experience a renewal of our faith. As our journey resumes, the circle repeats. We are like spiritual yo-yos. Well, at least I can be.

This stirring begins as a yearning for something more. We are all ordinary people facing Mount Everest. No pretense. No boasting. Just prayer and faith in God. I found my faith is fueled not from the power of my prayers—but from the One who hears it!

Thank you, redeeming Father,
that you desperately yearn to hear from me.
As I share all my cares and anxieties,
comfort me and provide peace.
Help me not be a spiritual yo-yo.
Set my focus always on you,
both through the good and the hard times.

March 10
Unconditional Surrender

The one who keeps God's commands lives in him,
and he in them.
And this is how we know that he lives in us:
We know it by the Spirit he gave us.
~ 1 John 3:24

When the Holy Spirit comes into us at our invitation, we receive as much of him as we will ever have. We do not get a little bit of him then and a little bit more in later experiences. Since the Spirit of God is a person, we cannot take him in pieces. He is an absolute. We either have *all* of the Holy Spirit or we have *none* of the Holy Spirit. Why is it, then, that we seem to give him only pieces of us? He comes to us unconditionally, yet we surrender to him conditionally.

For me, I gave him my Sundays but not my Mondays; that was my wash day and I was much too busy. I gave him my actions by playing the organ at church for years, but not my attitude. I gave him my friendships but not my reputation. I gave him my time but not my thoughts. I handed him my burdens (or so I thought) but not my body. I gave him my prayers but forgot my pleasures. I gave him my crises but not my children. I gave him my health but not my heart.

Then one day I stopped and asked myself, "Would you drop the conditions and give God all of you?" It was then that I gave God every minute of every day and entered into an intimate relationship with him. That decision changed me from the inside out. I wanted to give him everything!

Dear God, show me areas
where I haven't given everything to you.
Give me a total and future transformation in your heart.
I want to unconditionally surrender everything to you.

March 11
Thank You for Making My Heart New

He replied, "Because you have so little faith.
Truly I tell you,
if you have faith as small as a mustard seed,
you can say to this mountain,
'Move from here to there,' and it will move.
Nothing will be impossible for you."
~ Matthew 17:20

In the early church, Jesus's followers risked everything to believe that Jesus was the Messiah and the Son of God. When did God open your eyes to accept him as your Lord and Savior? Before I did that, I had so many questions. I didn't understand how the Divine and humanity could coexist in one person; it was beyond my understanding. For example, I knew that God has no beginning and cannot die. And that Jesus is God. Yet Jesus died. How can that be? He became a man, lived a perfect life, and veiled his glory in a human body, the garb of flesh.

Someone explained to me that if a prince leaves the royal palace to go and live in squalor and slums, although his position has changed, he is still the same person. Jesus came as a man so that he might die for humankind. It was the only way to save us and reconcile us to a holy God.

Recount the experience when God took your heart and made it new. That's your testimony. If you haven't done so yet, ask him into your heart. Confess your sins, and ask him to forgive you and become your Lord and Savior. There has never been a better time than *right now*. Thank him for his grace to make your heart new—beginning today.

Thank you, Lord,
for taking my heart and making it new.
I appreciate your grace.
Give me a way to share
with someone my testimony
of how you changed me.

March 12

Worship Is the "Thank You"
That Refuses to be Silenced

I will exalt you,
my God the King;
I will praise your name for ever and ever.
~ Psalm 145:1

Some people have tried to make science out of worship. I have found that can't be done any more than we can "sell love" or "negotiate peace" without God.

Worship is a voluntary act of gratitude offered by the saved to the Savior, by the healed to the Healer, and by the delivered to the Deliverer. It is the groaning of our spirit, our gratitude to our Savior that cannot be silenced.

After all, if Christ had not come, we and this world would indeed be without hope. If he had not died for humanity's redemption, we and this world would be lost. We would never be able to access God, there would be no atonement for sin, no forgiveness, and no eternal life, as there would be no Savior. We would be doomed to an eternity in hell and separated from God.

Call out to Jesus today for salvation and grace. Give him all the glory as you are doing mundane tasks. Sing praise songs while doing chores. In the solitude of your vehicle, belt out praise to the Lord. Even in your aloneness, worship your King of all creation. I always have praise music blasting throughout my home and car, as I always need a worship pick-me-up.

Remember, Jesus Christ came into the world and made it a better place. And he'll do the same for you—wherever you are, whatever you're doing, and whoever you are with.

Dear God, may a song of worship
to you always be on my lips.
May my heart overflow with your praise.
Pour into me as I seek you,
knowing you will always be found.

March 13
You Are My True Center

This hope is a strong and
trustworthy anchor for our souls.
~ Hebrews 6:19

God embodies all truth; therefore, He cannot lie. Our hope of heaven is secure and immovable, anchored in God, just as a ship's anchor holds firmly to the seabed. This truth should fill us with great peace.

Yet, I know how easy it is for my mind to wander from the Lord—especially when I'm sleep-deprived, stressed, or anxious. These are my personal warning signals, telling me I'm starting to drift. Like an anchor, the Holy Spirit gives me a gentle tug, prompting me to refocus on God's steady presence.

The closer we draw to God, the more attuned we become to our soul's anchor. When we approach him with openness, honesty, and sincerity, asking him to save us from our sins, he will do it. If this truth fills you with encouragement, assurance, and confidence, then grasp it with all your heart. Let God be your True Center, your unshakable anchor in every storm.

Lord, thank you for being my anchor,
secure and immovable.
When I feel myself drifting,
gently draw me back to you.
Help me to remain steadfast,
trusting in your truth
and unwavering love.
Be my True Center in all that I do.

March 14
Not Me, Lord—That's Impossible!

Now there was a believer in Damascus named Ananias.
The Lord spoke to him in a vision, calling, "Ananias!"
"Yes, Lord!" he replied.
"Go over to Straight Street, to the house of Judas.
When you get there, ask for a man from Tarsus named Saul.
He is praying to me right now."
~Acts 9:10–11

Let me set the scene. The Lord asked me to do something in faith—something that made me very uncomfortable. He told me to compile into a book all the devotionals I send out as texts. I wrestled with God repeatedly over this directive. I kept telling him that I'm not a writer. Finally, his Spirit spoke to my heart, "Not yet, but I am." Since that day, I've obeyed.

Like me, Ananias—an everyday believer with a deep love for God—was called by the Lord to play a pivotal role in launching the apostle Paul into his destiny for God's kingdom and his church. I want to be like Ananias. I want to be so in tune with God that he works through me daily, sharing his love and power with someone, somewhere, every day.

Now, imagine if we united in that same Spirit. What would happen if we committed to praying daily, with genuine faith, for our pastors, their families, and the church staff? Can you picture the ripple effects of such faithful intercession? The same God who blessed and empowered Paul is ready to bless and strengthen our church leaders today.

Lord, make me sensitive
to your voice and willing to be used like Ananias.
Unite us as a church to faithfully pray
for our leaders and to lift up one another in love.
May your power and blessings
flow through us to impact the world.

March 15

If My Heart Could Tell a Story

We are pressed on every side by troubles,
but we are not crushed.
We are perplexed,
but not driven to despair.
~ 2 Corinthians 4:8

About ten minutes into a fifty-five-minute drive, my heart felt like it might jump out of my chest. Then I felt like a butcher knife lodged in my back. "I think I'm having a heart attack!" I told my husband.

He calmly instructed me to pull the car over and switched places with me, then drove like a crazy person to the nearest hospital as he prayed that God would spare my life. On the way, he had me put an aspirin under my tongue, which made me horribly nauseated but probably saved my life.

Emergency heart catheterization showed my arteries to be totally clean, but I had a nasty blood clot blocking a major blood vessel supplying my heart—also known as a widow maker. Thankfully they were able to break up the clot, and the hospital released me a few days later with a new set of prescriptions, orders for rehab, and instructions to take it easy.

Now, less than a week after the ordeal, I am once again reminded that if I keep heaven in view, I can remain serene and cheerful even on the darkest of days. I feel more alive today than I have in years. It took this one major encounter with the clutches of death for me to fully understand how fleeting life really is.

Whether today is filled with pleasure or pain, we must see it for what it is—temporary. Earthly happiness and heartache pale in comparison with the treasures that await us in glory.

Dear Father God, thank you
for each day and moment that we live and breathe.
Help us make the most of each day
and not take any for granted.

March 16

A Spring for the Soul

For you are the fountain of life,
the light by which we see.
~ Psalm 36:9

Sadly, many people only feel happiness when everything is going great. If their lives are untroubled, they feel happy. But when difficulties abound, a relationship breaks down, or illness strikes, then happiness flees.

I find myself in this boat. When I get downcast, I relive my past traumas that have caused me grief and pain. I actively try to avoid suffering at all costs, living in fear of being hurt again.

Jesus promises *his peace* to all who trust in him. His well is overflowing with peace, as whoever drinks the water he gives them will never thirst: "Indeed, the water I give them will become in them a spring of water welling up to eternal life" (John 4:14 NIV).

Our Savior further tells us that "My peace I leave with you; my peace I give you. I do not give to you as the world gives. Do not let your hearts be troubled and do not be afraid" (John 14:27 NIV). The world attempts to woo people with its own description of happiness and peace. Today, spend time alone with Christ and experience *real joy*. See yourself completely safe, with your feet upon a rock and established in the ways of God.

> *My Great Defender, when I am faced with battles*
> *in this life, may I call out to you,*
> *trusting fully you will answer.*
> *You are the spring for my soul.*
> *I rest in your peace.*

March 17
A Wrong Turn...

Lately, I have struggled with thinking that God will withhold his mercy when I take the wrong path. It's like I forget all of God's promises found in his Word.

God is trustworthy. He is my hiding place, a fortress. So why do I allow thoughts of failure to invade my mind?

Perhaps you've taken a wrong turn or made a bad decision, and you are now experiencing the consequences. Maybe you, like me, are expecting God to withhold his eternal mercy until you get back on the straight and narrow and become perfect.

We have a Father God who has sent his Son to take the punishment for every sin we have ever committed and will commit.

Our eternal Daddy keeps all of our wanderings and catches each tear we cry. When we begin to grasp the depth of that truth, we can say with confidence, just as David did, "This I know: God is on my side" (Psalm 56:9).

The Lord is our wall of defense. Our great God is the one who delivers us. Our King is the one who gives us the comfort and strength we need to be courageous and endure.

Your heavenly Father knows your every struggle and will *never* leave your side, despite any wrong turns you make.

Dear God, thank you for never giving up on me.
Thank you for never leaving me nor forsaking me.

March 18
A Reunion to Look Forward To

Many Samaritans from the village believed in Jesus
because the woman had said, "He told me everything I ever did!"
. . . Then they said to the woman,
"Now we believe, not just because of what you told us,
but because we have heard him ourselves.
Now we know he is indeed the Savior of the world."
~ John 4:39, 42

We know the story well. The Samaritan woman immediately tells everyone she knows about her experiences with the Savior of the world. Despite her reputation of being married five times and living with a man who she was not married to, many of her fellow townspeople went to Jesus to hear his messages of truth, love, and the kingdom to come.

The good news is that Jesus changes everyone that he comes in contact with. If he can reach the woman at the well, he can transform us. What a day it will be when we get to reunite with all the believers in heaven.

Recently, I was blessed to celebrate my fiftieth class reunion with ten of my beloved classmates. Quite a few of them I get to see regularly, and others I have not seen for at least fifty years. Shocked, we all interacted as if we hadn't been apart for over five decades. It was like we had just seen each other as high school teenagers.

Jesus doesn't waste a thing, including all our difficulties and sins. He uses our past experiences, including our past mistakes, as opportunities to bring others to saving knowledge of him. What a reunion it will be when all of Jesus's followers join him in heaven.

Dear God, use everything in my life
to bring others to saving knowledge of you.
Give me the courage to share my testimony.
Use it to spread the gospel and
increase your kingdom.

March 19

Visualize That Deeper Dimension

Even when I walk through the darkest valley
I will not be afraid,
for you are close beside me.
Your rod and your staff protect and comfort me.
~ Psalm 23:4

As children of God, we are never alone! So many times I have questioned God's presence, especially during my darkest hours. But looking back, I now see that was when my Father was closest to me.

Our Shepherd is always with us. We never have to call him; he is already there. We don't have to fear that if things become too difficult, he will abandon us. He goes before us, walks beside us, and comes behind us. Just as our mighty Protector sees every sparrow and knows every hair that is on our heads (Luke 12:6–7), his gaze is constantly upon us.

Our Savior is so near to us, reassuring us throughout the journey that he still loves us and will remain with us. As this Lenten season approaches, remember to pray for and reach out to our leaders and those who are in tremendous pain, great sorrow, and anxiety, overcome with earthly fears.

It is only with Jesus that we can grasp that deeper dimension of the depth of love God has for us. Even though we walk through the darkest valley, we will not fear, knowing that he protects us.

Merciful God, redirect my spiritual eyes
to gaze upon those special souls who are struggling.
Give me eyes to see who you would want me
to pray for and bless during this season.
Instill in me a spirit of overwhelming
gratitude to you.

March 20

Walk by Faith, Not by Sight

Jesus replied,
"You don't understand now what I am doing,
but someday you will."
~ John 13:7

I became captivated by a documentary the other night. A sixty-year-old woman was determined to complete her bucket list by scaling a huge mountain cliff. Because of her story and our age similarity, I thought of my own mountains—none of which are physically dangerous.

In the last couple of years, I have found myself justifying my fears and explaining to God how worried I am about my cliffs. Every time, I leave my prayer conversation with my Father convicted. If only I would listen to him, my path might take an abrupt turn, leading me away from my personal uphill battles. Should I have to tackle any mountain, God has assured me, he will equip me thoroughly for the strenuous climb.

March 20

All God requires of us is to follow him one step at a time. We make it much harder by not trusting him. God's desire is for us to keep our minds on the present journey, all the while enjoying his presence.

As followers of Christ, we *get* to walk by faith and not by sight—trusting our Father to open the way before us.

Dear God, I feel like it's time
for me to reflect on my life and take inventory.
You know everything about me.
Please cleanse my soul from all fear.
You know every part of me and my future.
I trust you.

March 21
More Than Removing Dirt, Jesus Removes Doubt

I tell you the truth,
anyone who welcomes my messenger
is welcoming me,
and anyone who welcomes me
is welcoming the Father who sent me.
~ John 13:20

Can you imagine it? The One with the towel and basin is the King of the universe. Hands that shaped the stars now wash away the filth from the long roads the disciples traveled. Fingers that formed mountains now massaged dirty toes.

I imagine my response would be the same as Peter's as Jesus approached: "'You will never ever wash my feet!' Jesus replied, 'Unless I wash you, you won't belong to me.' Simon Peter exclaimed, 'Then wash my hands and head as well, Lord, not just my feet!'" (John 13:8–9). How often do we think we are not worthy of Jesus's cleansing and calling?

In Jesus's day, the washing of feet was a task reserved not just for servants but for the lowest of slaves. The Jewish slaves or servants could not wash people's feet, only Gentiles. It was equivalent to changing an adult's diaper. The streets in biblical times were heavy-laden with animal excrement and grime.

Hours before his own torture and death, Jesus's main concern was his disciples. He wanted them to know how much he loved them. More than removing dirt, Jesus removed their doubt of following him, of what he must do on the cross, and even of his divinity. Through this beautiful and humble illustration, he gives them their marching orders of what to do after his death on the cross. He washes away all of our doubts in following him.

Living Christ, you offered me mercy before I sought it. Forgive me, Lord, for questioning you.
May I always live with
no doubts about your calling on my life.

March 22
All for Us

My old self has been crucified with Christ.
It is no longer I who live, but Christ lives in me.
So I live in this earthly body by trusting in the Son of God,
who loved me and gave himself for me.
~ Galatians 2:20

Jesus Christ was crucified alongside two thieves on a rugged cross at Calvary, just outside Jerusalem. The very thought of the Son of God coming down from heaven and humbling himself in obedience to the point of death upon that instrument of Roman torture gives me chills.

Jesus gave his head to a painful crown of thorns for us. He gave his face for humans to spit upon in place of ours. He gave his cheeks to be beaten and his beard to be plucked out for us. He gave his back to be shredded by a whip laced with shards of metal and rocks in substitution for ours. He gave his side to be pierced by a Roman spear for us. He gave his hands and feet to spikes driven straight into flesh and bone for us. And his blood spilled out for payment for our sins.

Is that too graphic for you? What if this had been the end of the story? There would be no Holy Week, no Easter, and no hymns of triumph proclaiming, "Jesus Christ has risen today."[1]

For those who come to God through the Son, Jesus Christ, rejoice. Jesus now lives and intercedes for each of us.

I praise you, my risen Lord Jesus Christ,
for paying the price that my actions never could.
Thank you for dying for me
so that I can now be
reconciled with a holy God.

March 23
Safe to Believe

When everything is ready,
I will come and get you,
so that you will always
be with me where I am.
~ John 14:3

For three days, Jesus's body lay in that tomb. It did not rest, mind you. The Bible tells us that after he was put to death in the flesh, he was made alive by the Spirit and preached to imprisoned and disobedient spirits (see 1 Peter 3:19–20). Next, there was a stirring deep within the grave, and our loving Messiah stepped forth.

Then everything changed.

Jesus was raised from the dead.

We were declared righteous.

The resurrection was like an exploding flare announcing to all seekers that it is safe to believe.

Safe to believe in eternal bodies.

Safe to believe in heaven as our estate and the earth as its front porch.

Safe to believe in a time when fear won't keep us awake and pain won't keep us down.

Safe to believe in open graves and endless days of genuine praise.

Now everything was changed. Death used to be the end; now it is the beginning.

> *Righteous God, help me remember*
> *it is always safe to have faith.*
> *When I waver,*
> *make me strong*
> *to believe in the power of the cross.*

March 24
Why Did He Have to Die?

The message of the cross is foolish
to those who are headed for destruction!
But we who are being saved
know it is the very power of God.
~ 1 Corinthians 1:18

Until we come face-to-face with the true depth of human sin, we cannot fully comprehend the weight of Christ's sacrifice. It was not merely Pilate, Judas, or the crowd that sent Jesus to the cross; it was our sin. The suffering we witness in this world—the desolation of war, the gnawing ache of loneliness, the cry of the orphan, and the despair of the widow—all speak of a creation marred by sin.

This is why Jesus died.

He died for me and you.

Humanity's bitter cup of sin was what he drank, enduring the cross for our sake. Even in his most agonizing moment, he prayed,

"My Father! If it is possible, let this cup of suffering be taken away from me. Yet I want your will to be done, not mine" (Matthew 26:39).

As we reflect during this Easter season, in the midst of bunnies, easter eggs, and chocolate candies, may we each strive to live under the authority of God's Word and experience his daily blessings. The cross is not only a symbol of suffering; it is also the ultimate display of God's power to redeem.

Eternal Father, may the message of the cross
become a living truth that
empowers and guides me every day.
May I strive to live
by the authority of your Word
and enjoy your blessings daily.

March 25

God Is Still in the Resurrection Business

And God will raise us from the dead by his power,
just as he raised our Lord from the dead.
~ 1 Corinthians 6:14

Is there something in your life that seems dead? Do you fear something? Or are you terrified that someone is too far gone? When my heart travels to these dark places, I find a quiet corner of my mind. I envision a garden, feel the fresh spring wind brushing across my face, and see the morning light illuminating from the opening of the holy sepulcher. Merely a bystander, I am captivated by my King's tomb, which radiates such brightness.

The tormenting anguish from earlier disappears as the brilliance from Jesus Christ's burial vault overtakes all my thoughts. A newly transformed reminder of celestial light from the Holy Spirit puts everything into eternal perspective as I lay all my cares of death, or of a dear one being lost in a sea of blackness, gently on the altar of my King.

As I sit in silence, my eyes, mind, and emotions are once again focused on the holy tomb. A warmth of eternal power, light, and peace washes over me. The feeling of death that overwhelmed me moments ago is now replaced with a newness of life and rebirth. Jesus's resurrection changed all that forever. "Because I live, you will also live" (John 14:19 NIV).

Holy Spirit, breathe fresh life
into places that once held the stench of death
as I focus on the great power that raised
Jesus from the dead and is in me.

March 26

The Cross Is Always Enough

> "And they will not need to teach their neighbors,
> nor will they need to teach their relatives, saying,
> 'You should know the LORD.'
> For everyone, from the least to the greatest,
> will know me already," says the LORD.
> "And I will forgive their wickedness,
> and I will never again remember their sins."
> ~ Jeremiah 31:34

You will never know true happiness until you have established a true friendship with God. This is impossible apart from the cross of his Son, Jesus Christ. Jesus even interceded on our behalf: "Father, forgive them; for they do not know what they are doing" (Luke 23:34 NASB). Jesus suffered and died for *all of our sins* on the cross of Calvary, but only those of us who admit our sins and accept Jesus Christ as our Savior can have a relationship with the Father.

Why is this? Only through Christ's death on the cross can we be forgiven and reconciled to God. What is the first step? We must find a quiet place where each of us can meet and visit him alone. Next, we must repent of our sins and let him know we are going to trust him fully—not partially.

Warning: beware of human pride! Admitting to anyone that I am a sinner or that I am too weak to save myself makes me nauseated. But convicted by the Holy Spirit, I realize that I need to start somewhere. Only when we leave our pride at the cross can our hearts be open to our Redeemer's grace. Once we have opened our hearts to him, the Divine Bookkeeper cancels our sin debt in full! The cross is always enough.

Thank you, almighty God,
for canceling my sin debts once and for all.
I praise your holy name.
Be near to me and my loved ones
this Easter season.
Let us see you in a new way.

March 27

A Chance to Hear Her Once More

For this world is not our permanent home;
we are looking forward to a home yet to come.
~ Hebrews 13:14

Paul looked forward to death with great anticipation. He said, "For to me, to live is Christ, and to die is gain" (Philippians 1:21).

For as long as I can remember, every Easter, a petite, Christ-loving woman angelically sang "The Holy City" to a standing-room-only First Presbyterian Church sanctuary. As I proudly listened to my mother, Helen Marie (don't think I ever told her how proud I was of her), sing as if her very life depended on it, not a dry eye was visible. Not one.

Death for Paul was not an enemy to be feared but a reality to be welcomed in God's time. The end of his life was a joyous gateway to new life: eternity in heaven. Without the resurrection of Christ, we could have no hope for the future. The Bible promises that someday we are going to stand face-to-face with the resurrected Christ. All our questions will be answered, and all our sorrows and fears will vanish.

Death, for a Christian, is not the end; it is only the beginning! I'm assured I will see and hear my darling mother as she greets me as I cross that eternal threshold. And I will witness to the entire Holy City when I tell her, "Mom, I've always been so proud of you!"

Dear God, please bless and consecrate me
as I embark on my journey to the new city.
I am grateful for being called to this holy purpose
and new state of life, and for the grace to hear your voice.
Thank you.

March 28

Don't Leave Jesus on the Cross

Then the angel spoke to the women.
"Don't be afraid!" he said.
"I know you are looking for Jesus, who was crucified."
~ Matthew 28:5

On the third day after Christ's death, there was a great earthquake, and an angel of the Lord descended from heaven and came and rolled the stone away.

There have been moments in my life when I felt my Redeemer had deserted me. Deep in prayer and anguish, I would employ my Savior, "Lord, didn't you hear me cry out?"

Of course Jesus heard me. Usually, this is the time when God is stretching us in our faith. As I look back on the darkest times of my life when my Father seemed the quietest, those were the very times of my greatest spiritual growth.

The world has heard the greatest message: "He is not here; for he is risen" (Matthew 28:6). Those few words changed the history of the universe. Darkness and despair died. Hope and anticipation were born in the hearts of all humanity. Joy and new life now dawn in the hearts of all who believe.

Make no mistake, the expense of the cross was beyond extravagant. In our humanity, it is beyond our capacity to pay for what Jesus did on the cross for us. It would bankrupt us to even consider the price. Jesus gave us an extravagant gift. And it wasn't easy. It was costly.

Be encouraged. Don't leave Jesus on the cross or in the tomb—for he is risen. Risen indeed. Your Savior is alive and walks beside you every day.

Lord, may I always be found seeking you,
knowing you hear my every cry and
have risen to meet my greatest need:
reconciliation with a holy God.
I am blessed.
Blessed indeed.

March 29
Sacred Delight

God blesses those who are poor and
realize their need for him,
for the Kingdom of Heaven is theirs.
~ Matthew 5:3

I recall one particularly tough season in my life when hope seemed elusive. I was going through a faith-challenging season, and the weight of my struggles felt overwhelming. One morning, as I walked outside feeling defeated, I noticed a tiny spring flower pushing through a crack in the pavement. That small, unexpected bloom reminded me of God's ability to bring life, beauty, and hope even in the hardest circumstances. It felt like a sacred delight—a heavenly joy that only God can provide.

Jesus told us to understand our need for God, and that in doing so, the kingdom of heaven becomes ours. This sacred delight is our good news. It's the kind of joy that feels too good to be true, yet it is. Knowing that God is not only our Defender and Father but also our pinch-hitter, lawyer, biggest fan, and best friend provides us with such comfort, even in our darkest days. This is when we find hope in the most unexpected places, like a flower pushing through a crack in life's harshest pavement.

This is the same sacred delight as the surprise that turned the dawn of Easter morning into a celebration of new life. We are the band of pilgrims that God promises a special blessing. We get to access this sacred delight to the kingdom—our heavenly joy—every day. As Christians, we get to make it an Easter sunrise every morning.

Dear Lord, when I'm faced with temptation,
turn my heart to prayer, worship,
or Scripture memorization instead of giving in.
Help me keep your sacred delight of the kingdom
in the forefront of my mind, especially
when I'm going through difficult times.
I trust you!

March 30

Very Much Like a Thief in the Night

I know all the things you do,
that you are neither hot nor cold.
I wish that you were one or the other!
But since you are like lukewarm water,
neither hot nor cold, I will spit you out of my mouth!
You say, "I am rich. I have everything I want.
I don't need a thing!"
And you don't realize that you are wretched and
miserable and poor and blind and naked.
~ Revelation 3:15–17

I once attended a breathtaking church service. The choir sang beautifully, the building gleamed, and the children's program ran like a well-oiled machine. Yet, something felt hollow. People went through the motions, but there seemed to be no genuine connection to the Spirit. It reminded me of a tree that looks healthy on the outside but is rotting within. That experience made me reflect on my own faith. Am I alive in Christ, or am I simply maintaining appearances?

God does not tolerate a mediocre spiritual walk, like that of the Laodicean church. Even though this church was thriving, wealthy, and self-sufficient, God rebuked them in this portion of Scripture. These strong words remind us that God cannot stomach a lukewarm church or faith.

Do you belong to such a church? Is your faith hot, cold, or lukewarm? During this season, let's reflect on our own personal relationship with Christ.

If each one of us were handed a sealed envelope from God on Easter Sunday, what would your note read? Would our Father express his gratitude for your love and service, or would he express his sadness by the false pretenses you display when coming into his presence?

Risen Christ, may I always rejoice and
spread your love and glory.
Make sure I am prepared for your return.
Make my faith burn hot and
never be lukewarm.

March 31

Lord, May I Always Be Found Seeking You

Then the angel spoke to the women.
"Don't be afraid!" he said.
"I know you are looking for Jesus,
who was crucified."
~ Matthew 28:5

Every year for the past several years, in preparation for Easter, my husband has asked me to sit with him and watch *The Passion of the Christ*. I knew I would struggle once again to witness the severe beatings Christ took in the courtyard in my place. This time, I chose to look for things missed in the past, like those filled with hatred. The Roman guards, the high priests, the bystanders who scorned and spat upon our bloodied and beaten beloved Son of the living God all grieved me. My heart ached as I watched my tortured Savior make the long trek to Golgotha surrounded by such intense persecution from those he came to save. Right afterward, I immediately went to my prayer closet and rededicated my sinful and dirty life—a first for me after watching the movie for years!

As I felt the weight of my unconfessed sin once again lifted from me, the Holy Spirit reminded me of my King's resurrection: "His appearance was like lightning, and his clothes were as white as snow. The guards were so afraid of him that they shook and became like dead men" (Matthew 28:3–4 NIV).

A new life now dawns in the hearts of all who believe.

Dear Lord and Savior,
thank you for suffering such a horrific death for me.
Thank you for taking the payment
for all of my sins on the cross
and reconciling me with a holy and perfect God.
I praise you for redeeming me
and all who believe in you as their Savior.
Help us never drift from your embrace.

April

April 1

Home at Last

The one sitting on the throne said,
"Look, I am making everything new!"
And then he said to me,
"Write this down,
for what I tell you is trustworthy and true."
~ Revelation 21:5

After three days of steady, refreshing rain, I stand in awe, gazing across the valley. For months, this landscape was nothing but an arid, dry, brown backdrop of the Chihuahuan Desert. Now, the same area is bursting with life, lush with green foliage and newly laid well-manicured fairways of a golf course. The transformation is astonishing, and I am reminded of God's promise that he makes all things new (see Revelation 21:5).

No artist's depiction of heaven can truly capture its splendor. Not long after my daughter's double lung transplant, she shared with us an extraordinary experience. One night, Jesus Christ visited her.

She described each intricate detail of our Savior—from the most penetrating eyes to a beautiful and unforgettable voice that dripped love. He took her on a journey, granting her an afternoon in heaven. The amount of vivid details she shared with us could fill books! She spoke of an endless field of golden-yellow flowers, their colors so rich they defied earthly comparison. Then a divine fragrance filled the air as the Lamb of God led her through radiant streets. This sweetness permeated all of heaven, making it both beautiful and complete.

Carmen's story was more than a testimony; it was a gift. She stirred in me a deep sense of longing—a homesickness to be "home at last."

Lord, help me to hold onto
that hope that we are only visitors here on earth,
and let that truth guide me daily
as I look forward to the day
when I am truly home.

April 2

Just Another Prayer Meeting

Your wickedness will bring its own punishment.
Your turning from me will shame you.
You will see what an evil,
bitter thing it is to abandon the Lord your God and
not to fear him.
I, the Lord, the Lord of Heaven's Armies,
have spoken!
~ Jeremiah 2:19

On the way home from a prayer meeting years ago, I realized how much of the evening felt scripted—repeated phrases, familiar requests, and a hurried pace to finish on time. I remember mindlessly nodding along, not truly connecting with the Lord. That night, a sense of emptiness crept over me. Had I actually communed with my Father, or had I just gone through the motions? That realization led me to invite God back into what had become a hollow routine.

Christianity is meant to be an intimate, growing relationship with Jesus Christ, not merely a checklist of doctrines, practices, and sins to avoid. God designed worship and prayer for us to encounter him in all his glory, not to become another "religious" obligation.

Prayer was given to us as a means to converse with God, yet how often do we rush through our prayers and then move on without pausing to listen to our Abba? Religious actions that lack genuine connection with God become empty rituals, like "just another prayer meeting." We don't want to be like the people in Jeremiah's time who were content with going through the motions, satisfied with the formality even when God's presence was absent.

Let us not settle for a hollow religious life. We need to actively pursue a vibrant, personal relationship with Jesus Christ. When God is truly present, the difference is undeniable.

Heavenly Father, reveal your desires for my life.
Remove any thought or action
that draws me away from you,
and lead me into deeper communion
with your heart.

April 3
It's That Time of Year Again!

I have learned to be content whatever the circumstances.
I know what it is to be in need,
and I know what it is to have plenty.
I can do all things through Christ
who gives me strength.
~ Philippians 4:11–13

Here it comes again. About this time every year, when spring is right around the corner, I get an incredible itch to clean out every closet, wash windows inside and out, dust all light fixtures, and, if possible, complete my tasks within twenty-four hours. I turn into a crazed cleaning woman! I'm exhausted just thinking about all I do in a day to complete my spring cleaning.

Why is it that we keep working harder for something bigger and greater? By the time we are in midlife, we might feel we have missed the mark on something really great and wonder whether this is all there is in life. Maybe my insatiable need for cleaning reflects my desire to be righteous in my deeds and not depend on Christ for my salvation?

Thankfully, God made me to be uncomplicated in my faith. My goals, second to honoring God, are to watch my children grow up, to learn how to listen, and to lend a helping hand regardless of who people are or how they look. God made us to be authentic, to become our own best person and not compare ourselves to others.

> *Dear God, help me not try to accomplish*
> *my entire to-do list in one day.*
> *Encourage me to reset, relax,*
> *and breathe in your grace*
> *and love.*

April 4
Think Before You Speak!

The tongue can bring death or life;
those who love to talk will reap the consequences.
~ Proverbs 18:21

This verse hit me hard this morning and brought back painful and embarrassing memories. When my daughters were little, there were times when they suffered a barrage of hurtful words when my temper got the better of me. I can only hope and pray that those moments have faded from their recollections.

My struggle with controlling my tongue started early, and my parents would be the first to confirm that if they were alive today. God, in his wisdom, always led me back to Scripture and repentance at just the right moment, reminding me of the importance of my words.

Our words carry tremendous power. They have the potential to affect others deeply, influencing hearts and shaping lives. Because words carry weight, we must be vigilant about what we say. The goal should be to use our words to encourage and build up, not to tear down. We all know the sting of hurtful words spoken about us and to us. Let's choose not to inflict that pain on others. To consistently make that choice, we need the daily help and guidance of the Holy Spirit.

> *Redeeming Father, I know how inadequate*
> *I am to be both judge and jury.*
> *Grant me a heart full of compassion so that*
> *I can reflect your love in my words and actions.*

April 5

You Need Never Leave the House of God

Seek the Kingdom of God above all else, and live righteously,
and he will give you everything you need.
"So don't worry about tomorrow,
for tomorrow will bring its own worries.
Today's trouble is enough for today."
~ Matthew 6:33–34

I remember a day when life's worries seemed relentless. The deadlines at work were piling up, my to-do list at home was never-ending, and an unexpected car repair pushed me over the edge. Sitting in traffic that evening, I felt my frustration start to boil over. And then a small, quiet voice reminded me, "You're in my presence, even here." It was then I realized that I didn't need a quiet corner or a church pew to connect with God; his house is with me wherever I am.

Worry adds nothing to our lives. When you find yourself stuck in traffic, step into his sanctuary. When life's gusts of temptation make you feel unsteady, take refuge behind the wall of his strength. If you work alongside people who belittle or discourage you, imagine sitting on a porch swing next to your heavenly Father, where he comforts and reassures you. This isn't a house of stone, nor will you find it in any real estate listing.

You'll find it in Scripture. I challenge each of us to do something different this year—to live in it. View it as the floor plan of our spiritual home. God provides the blueprint for each of us.

In these verses, Jesus offers more than a template for prayer; he invites us to live daily in his presence, whether in traffic, at work, on lunch dates, at school, piloting a plane, or driving an eighteen-wheeler.

Wonderful Counselor, I long to be in your presence,
giving, praying, and worshiping.
Keep me there despite the challenges of life
and pain swirling around me.

April 6
The Tale of the Women at the Tomb

Teach these new disciples to
obey all the commands I have given you.
And be sure of this:
I am with you always, even to the end of the age.
~ Matthew 28:20

Both Marys and Joanna knew they had a task before them. Even though Joseph and Nicodemus had wrapped their Savior for burial in spices, they didn't have time before the Sabbath to properly anoint his body. These women were on a mission. Their Lord, Savior, and Teacher needed to be anointed for burial.

The other disciples were hiding in a room, terrified of the Roman soldiers. After all, their leader had just been crucified. But these women decided to risk everything to properly care for their Lord. Whether or not they were tempted to give up, I'm so glad they didn't.

We know the Father was watching them. I'm sure God was smiling at their hearts to care for his Son.

These women received the blessing, as they were the first ones to witness the resurrection of the Savior of the World. Our God loves surprising us with his miracles. And he is still doing it today. The tomb could not hold his Son. Just when her womb seemed too old for babies, Sarah got pregnant. Just when the failure seemed too great for grace, David was forgiven of his sins. And when the road was too dark at the grave of the Savior, these women were changed *forever* by seeing their risen Lord *first*.

The lesson? Don't give up, and don't quit! For if you do, you may miss the answer to your prayers. God is still a God of miracles. He still moves stones.

Risen Lord, may I never be too preoccupied,
busy, or lazy to put off the blessing that awaits me.
May I continue to trust in you,
my God of miracles.

April 7

Christ Provides the Cure

This means that anyone who belongs to
Christ has become a new person.
The old life is gone; a new life has begun!
~ 2 Corinthians 5:17

I often catch myself looking for quick fixes—a new cream, a supplement, or anything that promises to turn back the clock without the effort of running those miles on the treadmill. Who wouldn't love an easy solution that promises to restore youth and vitality?

Seriously, wouldn't it be wonderful if we could find a medicine that would absolutely cure human nature's weaknesses and failures? Conflict, discontent, and unhappiness plague people everywhere. But suppose we could come up with a cure? It would cause a worldwide stampede!

Here's the most amazing news: that cure already exists. Christ is the answer. Through him, our sins are forgiven, and by the power of the Holy Spirit, our lives are transformed and renewed. The old life, with its sins and confusion, is replaced by righteousness, joy, and hope. It's in Christ that our souls find true peace—a peace that no product on a shelf could ever deliver.

This is so encouraging for those of us who want the instant change promised in a bottle screaming youth or happiness. Remember that what God offers is so much more. Our Redeemer brings complete renewal from the inside out, an eternal change that no quick fix could ever match.

Father God, create in me a clean heart
and renew a right spirit within me.
Help me to seek true renewal
through you alone.

April 8

Look Beyond the Pain
to Find God's Purpose

Now may the God of peace—who brought up from the dead
our Lord Jesus, the great Shepherd of the sheep,
and ratified an eternal covenant with his blood—
may he equip you with all you need for doing his will.
May he produce in you, through the power of Jesus Christ,
every good thing that is pleasing to him.
All glory to him forever and ever!
~ Hebrews 13:20–21

He heard you. He saw you. Christ saw your face the very moment you first believed, your eyes filled with newfound hope. The same face that greets you in the mirror each morning was the face he saw, and that was enough for him to choose the cross. He left his heavenly throne for you, for me. Jesus, the perfect example of faith and obedience, surrendered all—even to death—because he could not stand to see us lost in hopelessness.

Jesus set aside the security of his earthly life, laying down his carpenter's hammer. He hung up his apron and closed the wooden shutters of his workshop, stepping out onto a path that led to unimaginable suffering. Why? Because his love for us outweighed the comfort he left behind. Yes, he left his comfort zone because of us!

I have often wondered, *Did he ever wish to stay?* He knew the end of the story. If there was any hesitation on the part of his humanity, it was overcome by the compassion of his divinity. This realization makes me pause and marvel at the depth of his sacrifice.

Dear God, help me to see beyond the pain of my struggles
and find joy even in difficult times,
just as Jesus did.
Prepare my heart
to understand your purpose for me,
and thank you for your
boundless love.

April 9
So Why Act Like It?

For every child of God defeats this evil world,
and we achieve this victory through our faith.
~ 1 John 5:4

I remember a time when I felt completely overwhelmed. A series of setbacks left me feeling vulnerable and isolated. I convinced myself that I had to handle everything on my own, and I quickly became exhausted trying to do so. It wasn't until a friend reminded me, "You know you're not alone in this, right? You have God," I finally turned to God with my whole heart. Instantly, I felt the power of surrender, and I was reminded that I never had to fight alone; God was there, arms open, ready to equip me.

One of Satan's most deceptive tactics is making us believe we have to face our struggles alone. He whispers that the weight is ours to carry, that the battle is ours to fight without any help. But God sees our needs and offers his strength and support.

The Bible warns us, "Be sober, be vigilant; because your

adversary the devil walks about like a roaring lion, seeking whom he may devour" (1 Peter 5:8 NKJV). Imagine for a moment coming face-to-face with an actual lion. Your natural response would be to defend yourself.

The good news? God has already provided the tools we need to fend off the enemy. His Word is our sword. His angels stand guard over us. His Spirit empowers us, and we find support in the prayers and encouragement of fellow believers. When evil and temptation approach, we can flee to the safety of God's provision. Since we aren't in this battle alone, why do we act like it? God's love is steadfast and everlasting, providing us with all we need to stand firm.

> *Were it not for your love, God, I would be lost.*
> *Thank you for your unfailing support*
> *and the victory you promise through faith.*
> *Help me remember that*
> *I never face these battles alone.*

April 10
How High Is Your Wall?

In your strength I can crush an army;
with my God I can scale any wall.
~ Psalm 18:29

The Bible confronts us with our moral independence within ourselves and our spiritual dependence on God. As only David can describe, "By my God, I can leap over a wall" (Psalm 18:29 ESV). God has not left us powerless. However, when I've tried to jump over ramparts of affliction, a wayward child, a financial bind, or a drought, I repeatedly fall short.

I remember a season when my family faced significant financial challenges. Every day felt like scaling a brick barricade that grew taller as unexpected expenses piled up. I did everything I could think of—tightened the budget, added additional sources of income—but the strain remained. I was exhausted and frustrated, feeling as though every effort ended in failure. It wasn't until one night, after an anxious prayer where I laid everything before God, that we received an unexpected phone call with an opportunity that changed everything. It was at that moment I understood that with God's strength, I could face and overcome even the highest walls.

What obstacles do you need to clear? Is it a habit that holds you captive or an emotion that constantly defeats you? Maybe it's a health scare, a wayward child, or an overwhelming sense of depression. The enemy would love for us to believe these barriers are impossible to overcome. But remember, when we align with God's power, nothing is impossible (see Luke 1:37).

God of the universe, like David,
I believe that with you,
I can leap over any wall.
Yet, when my walls seem higher
than I can manage, remind me
that I can do nothing without your strength.
Cover me with your undeniable power, Lord.

April 11

For the Worrier

The Lord is close to all who call on him,
yes, to all who call on him in truth.
~ Psalm 145:18

Think about all the things you never worry about. I don't spend a moment wondering whether water will flow from my bathroom faucet—until the day I turn it on and nothing comes out. I don't worry about a tree falling on my house, at least not until a storm shakes the heavy branches outside my window.

This past weekend, we celebrated a family birthday at an outdoor event with thousands of people gathered, thick as crickets. Years ago, I would have joined the fun without a second thought. But now, with my grandchildren running and the music thundering so loudly that I could barely think, worry crept in. I started fretting about everything from everyone's safety to losing sight of the kids—things that usually wouldn't cross my mind.

Even if you're a natural worrier, there are still some things you don't concern yourself with. Take a moment to ask yourself, *Why do some concerns dominate my thoughts while others don't even register?*

We can be just as certain and worry-free about God's love and protection in *all* things. The greatest proof of this is the cross, where God showed the depth of his love for each of us. He has never broken a promise, so why would he start now?

Faithful Lord, you are an ever-present source
of strength in my life.
Grant me the patience and resilience
to face even the smallest challenges
today with unwavering trust.

April 12
Our Lives Require His Presence

That's why I take pleasure in my weaknesses,
and in the insults, hardships, persecutions,
and troubles that I suffer for Christ.
For when I am weak, then I am strong.
~ 2 Corinthians 12:10

Have you ever noticed how different God's idea of strength is from ours? The Lord told Paul, "My power is made perfect in weakness" (2 Corinthians 12:9 ESV). Paul discovered that only by admitting his frailty and getting out of God's way could his Father powerfully work through him and in the situation.

I've experienced this firsthand. When I attempt to accomplish God's will by relying solely on my strength, the results are minimal, often insignificant. But when I surrender, allowing God to take over, his strength shines through. His presence brings fulfillment and deep satisfaction that human effort alone could never achieve.

April 12

I wonder whether things would be easier if the next time we feel weak or inadequate for the task God has set before us, we remember that the Lord's strength is perfected in our surrender. As we pray with an open heart, trust in his provision, and be ready to serve as he leads, we can experience his peace firsthand.

Faithful God, thank you
for showing your strength in my weakness.
Help me trust in your presence and power
so that I can serve you fully and bring glory to your name.
Give me the grace to not trust in my own strength,
but to rely solely on yours.
Bless me with your peace
as I trust in you.

April 13
No Cliffhanger

Now Christ has gone to heaven.
He is seated in the place of honor next to God,
and all the angels and authorities
and powers accept his authority.
~ 1 Peter 3:22

Faith in Christ isn't a leap into uncertainty. It is built on the solid facts of his life, death, and resurrection. Consider the evidence: Christ lived a perfect life, challenging those around him with, "Which of you convicts me of sin?" (John 8:46 ESV), and none could respond. His death was foretold by the prophets hundreds of years before he was born, fulfilling every detail with divine precision.

The resurrection is an undeniable testament to his power, evidenced by transformed lives throughout history. In Christ alone lies the power to change human hearts—and he continues to do so every moment of every day.

There was a time when I felt like I was standing on the edge of a cliff. It was a season of doubt, one where the future seemed uncertain. I clung to the promise that Christ's life and resurrection were not just stories but realities that meant my life was secure in him. In those moments, I felt his peace wash over me, reassuring me that my faith wasn't based on wishful thinking but on solid truth.

As believers, we are called to follow his example of servanthood, a living testimony of our new life in him. This calling is not left in suspense, as we know the rest of the story. For those who choose not to listen, the edge of the cliff remains.

Lord, help me leave behind the old ways
and embrace a life grounded
in your unwavering love and power.
Guide me to live by your standards
and reflect your truth.

April 14
A Vital Lesson

John said to Jesus,
"Teacher, we saw someone using your name
to cast out demons,
but we told him to stop because
he wasn't in our group."
~ Mark 9:38

When I was a child, the first week of June at Vacation Bible School marked the start of summer for me. Each morning began with the song "This Little Light of Mine," complete with hand motions and enthusiastic voices. I never imagined that a simple tune would carry such meaning into my adult life. Yet, it did—its message echoed in my heart for years to come.

We each hold a light that we are called to let shine, no matter how small it may seem. In a world full of darkness, even a flickering candle has power. Once, when I was faced with the temptation to keep my faith quiet, to blend in rather than stand out, remembering that simple song compelled me to let my light shine. That made a difference to those around me in ways I never anticipated.

Our lights may seem small in a world shadowed by hate and selfishness, but we must keep them burning. A single flame may appear insignificant, but when combined with others, it becomes an unstoppable force. God's plan for us is not to be lone beacons; we are meant to shine together as one body in Christ.

Holy Father, may I strive daily to be a light in the darkness.
Let my flame encourage others to join in,
so we may illuminate
the world together.

April 15

Christ Saves . . . Regardless
of Your Last Name

He is the faithful witness to these things,
the first to rise from the dead,
and the ruler of all the kings of the world.
All glory to him who loves us and
has freed us from our sins by shedding his blood for us.
~ Revelation 1:5

When multimillionaire tycoon J. P. Morgan passed away, it was revealed that his will spanned thirty-seven articles and nearly ten thousand words. His legacy was marked by monumental transactions and vast sums of wealth. By worldly measures, he was a giant among men, respected and admired. Yet, when it came to his soul's eternal destiny, not one penny could secure it. Just as the humble, dying thief on Calvary depended on God's grace, so do we all.

Years ago, this truth became clear to me. I was attending a community church service where people from every walk of life gathered; wealthy business owners sat next to those who struggled to make ends meet. That night, as we shared stories and sang hymns, I realized that no title, job, or inheritance could bridge the gap between us and God. Only God's love could, and it did. We were all there, humbled and grateful, held by the same grace that covered each of us equally.

It's often said that the ground is level at the foot of the cross. We all come, no matter our name or status, burdened by sin and needing redemption. And we all leave, not as we were but washed clean, equally forgiven, and equally cherished. The same sacrifice was made for each of us, from the mighty to the meek.

Mighty God, your love and mercy are without limit.
Thank you for the gift of salvation
that knows no rank or reputation.
Help me, Lord, to lean on your everlasting love
and find strength in your promise,
regardless of what I face.

April 16

Homeward Bound

Look, I am coming soon!
Blessed are those who obey
the words of prophecy written in this book.
~ Revelation 22:7

It's hard to watch things grow old. The town where I spent my childhood is a testament to time's passage—buildings that once bustled with life are now boarded up, and houses that once held laughter stand in disrepair or have been torn down altogether. My husband and I poured our hearts into the old mercantile building we bought years ago, but now its doors will soon close, signaling the end of a bittersweet chapter. Even the movie house where I spent countless evenings, once filled with warmth and excitement, now sits silent and cold. For a moment, sadness crept in as I realized how much had changed.

There are moments when I wish I could turn back the clock, brush the dust off the streets, and relive the days when everything felt vibrant and new. But no matter how strong that longing, I know it's beyond my reach. Yet, I take comfort in knowing there is One who can make all things new—God. As the shepherd once wrote, "He restores my soul" (Psalm 23:3 NASB).

God doesn't patch up or reform; he renews and restores completely. He will take the original blueprint and bring it back to life, breathing hope and energy into what once was. Thankfully, God's promise isn't tied to buildings or towns. It's tied to something greater—his power to restore hope and bring us to a future that outshines anything we've ever known.

Gentle Lamb, may I worship you and
speak of your amazing love.
When I encounter others,
lost or found, give me the courage
to share the future you have promised—
a future that renews, restores, and
makes all things new.

April 17

Even Greater Joy

We are here for only a moment,
visitors and strangers in the land as our ancestors
were before us.
Our days on earth are like a passing shadow,
gone so soon without a trace.
~ 1 Chronicles 29:15

Even at its most wonderful, life on earth is but a fleeting glimpse of what heaven holds. Does that mean we should distance ourselves from the joys this world offers? Not at all. Often, the blessings we experience are whispers of a greater promise, glimpses of what is to come. Moments like the joy of marriage, the birth of a child, or the warm embrace of a grandparent are more than just happiness; they are a hint of heaven's glory.

I still remember the awe and overwhelming joy that filled my heart when our daughters were born. The happiness seemed too perfect, as if life had reached its peak. And then, to our surprise, God blessed us again with two wonderful grandsons. Each milestone, each shared laugh, and every embrace reminded me that these blessings were merely a foretaste of an even greater joy waiting for us beyond this life.

There was a day when I stood in the garden with my grandsons, watching them chase butterflies and giggle in the sunshine. In this moment, my heart swelled with gratitude as I realized this was a glimpse of heaven's beauty and a small echo of what eternal joy would feel like. The Bible tells us, "Every good and perfect gift is from above, and comes down from the Father of lights" (James 1:17).

Oh, great Creator of all things beautiful and intricate,
I recognize that you are my greatest joy.
I offer my gratitude for the abundance
you have bestowed upon me,
and may I never forget to savor these moments,
for they are the promise of
even greater things to come.

April 18
Only Jesus Can Satisfy

In peace I will lie down and sleep,
for you alone,
O Lord, will keep me safe.
~ Psalm 4:8

Drug and alcohol addiction is one of the most pressing challenges of our time. It's not just illegal substances; many struggle with physical dependence on prescription medication just to make it through the day or to find rest at night. I'm not a doctor, and I understand that some medications have a rightful place when used under medical guidance. Yet, I can't help but think back to my teenage and college years, when too many friends sought solace in substances rather than God. They turned to drugs and alcohol as an escape, choosing temporary relief over facing their problems head-on with God's help.

The book of Proverbs speaks the truth when it says alcohol goes down smoothly but "bites like a serpent, and stings like a viper"

(Proverbs 23:32 NKJV). The momentary comfort fades, leaving behind lingering pain. I remember close friends in college who struggled with the lure of alcohol. At first, it was just at social gatherings, a way to unwind. But over time, it became more—a crutch, a daily need. I watched as its influence pulled them further from peace and deeper into a cycle that only brought destruction. It was a sobering reminder that nothing can substitute for the salvation of Jesus Christ.

Dear God, I know that true peace—
the kind that allows me to lie down
at night and sleep without worry—
comes from you alone.
Father, you know the depths of my struggles,
and you offer a path of real comfort,
not just fleeting moments.
May I always turn to you first and
find the peace that only your Son,
Jesus, can provide.

April 19

Just the Proper Proportion

Do not love this world nor the things
it offers you, for when you love the world,
you do not have the love of the Father in you.
~ 1 John 2:15

There was a time when I found myself caught up in pursuing achievements that seemed so important at the moment. It felt fulfilling at first, but gradually I realized how my priorities shifted. The drive to succeed clouded my heart and left little room for God. Then I understood how subtle worldliness can be, creeping in without notice until it takes root.

As Christians, we are warned not to fall in love with the world. Worldliness is more than just an attachment to material things—it is an attitude, a spirit, an atmosphere that saturates society. It puts self above all else, disregarding God and his commandments. It shows itself in countless ways: habits, selfish pleasures, the relentless pursuit of material gain, and ambition that comes at the expense of others.

We are called to discern between what brings genuine joy and what distracts us from God's truth. Pleasure itself isn't inherently wrong, but it becomes problematic when it is misused or it leads us away from the Lord.

We must stay vigilant, watching for any trace of worldliness that might creep into our lives. The Bible's reminder, "May the meditations of my heart be acceptable in your sight" (Psalm 19:14 ESV), serves as a touchstone, guiding us back to him whenever we stray.

Lord Jesus, I acknowledge that no comfort the world offers
can compare to your loving embrace.
Help me surrender each day into your care,
so that I may hold tightly to your truth
and let go of anything that distracts me from you.
Hold me close, and may I find my fulfillment
only in your presence.

April 20

The Greatest Gift

They were calling out to each other,
"Holy, holy, holy is the Lord of Heaven's Armies!
The whole earth is filled with his glory!"
~ Isaiah 6:3

The Bible teaches us that God is holy and pure. On the cross, as the weight of every human sin was laid upon him, Christ cried out, "My God, my God, why have you forsaken me?" (Matthew 27:46 NIV). In that unimaginable moment, Jesus bore the ultimate punishment for our sins, enduring the separation and suffering that should have been ours. It was a scene of profound anguish and love intertwined.

If we needed to make a list of the things we are grateful for, what would it include? Perhaps family, health, friends, and church? Those are wonderful answers, full of meaning and worth. But there is one gift that surpasses them all—God's gift of his Son, who willingly took on the penalty we deserved and brought us salvation.

April 20

Once, during a particularly difficult season when my life felt overwhelming, a friend reached out with a simple gesture—a handwritten note and prayer. That small act reminded me of Christ's gifts we are called to give and receive: the encouragement, kindness, and hope that reflect our Savior's love. It also brought to mind how often I've been blessed by others' generosity and support. This, too, is a reminder of the ultimate gift we've been given—one that inspires us to give and to share his love freely.

Heavenly Father, commission us to be your hands and feet,
telling others about your boundless wisdom
and the immeasurable depth of your love.
May our hearts be full of gratitude,
and may our lives reflect the incredible gift
you've given us in Jesus.

April 21
No Matter How Dark the Season

Give thanks to the Lord,
for he is good.
His faithful love endures forever.
~ Psalm 107:1

Separated from friends, unjustly accused, and subjected to brutal treatment—if anyone had a right to voice grievances, it was the apostle Paul. Yet instead of filling the cold, dark cell with complaints, his lips were full of praise and thanksgiving. Paul understood the meaning of true gratitude, even amid great suffering.

Close your eyes for a moment and picture that dark, cold cell. Now, listen closely. Can you hear Paul's voice rising, undeterred, making melody to the Lord, always giving thanks for all things in the name of our Lord Jesus Christ (see Ephesians 5:19–20)? Imagine the whispers of the guards and the prisoners around him. They might think the man in Paul's cell has lost his mind, yet this apostle's singing only grows stronger. For Paul, thanksgiving wasn't an annual or weekly ritual; it was a steadfast daily practice that fueled his joy, no matter the circumstances.

When I struggled in my grieving, I stumbled across Paul's story and was struck by his unwavering gratitude. Inspired, I began to write down at least one thing I was thankful for each day, even if it was small. Soon, I found my perspective shifting, my spirit lifted by the act of recognizing God's constant faithfulness, even in the midst of trials.

Oh Lord, my Savior and Deliverer,
I express my gratitude for lifting me from my struggles.
Your faithfulness and justice in forgiving me
are truly awe-inspiring.
May I learn to give thanks every day,
following Paul's example,
and trust in you.
Hallelujah!

April 22
The Most Remarkable Book in History

Keep on asking,
and you will receive what you ask for.
Keep on seeking,
and you will find.
Keep on knocking,
and the door will be opened to you.
~ Matthew 7:7

A little girl returned from her first day at school. When her mom asked, "Honey, did you learn anything?" the girl replied, "Apparently not enough. I have to go back tomorrow, the next day, and the day after that!" That response could easily have come from my eldest grandson.

We all need that reminder that learning is a journey, not a onetime event. And this is especially true when it comes to understanding the Bible. The first step to making the Bible come alive in our lives is to *pray* for understanding. *Ask* your eternal Father to speak to your heart through his Word and you will *receive* if it is in God's will.

The next step? *Seek, and you will find.* The Bible is like a hidden treasure, full of promises and wisdom waiting to be uncovered. Approach it with curiosity and dedication.

Finally, there's the third step: *Knock, and the door will be opened.* Be present and ready to act on what you learn. It's one thing to read and know; it's another to apply that knowledge to your life. When I'm searching for guidance during a difficult decision, I need to shift from *just reading* God's Word to *actively praying and seeking* my King until the peace I'm looking for finds me.

The truly joyful are those who not only read God's perfect law but continue to study and live by it. If we only skim the words but don't obey them, we'll miss out on the deep and abiding joy of the Lord. *Ask, seek,* and *knock*—it's that simple.

Dear God, help me seek you with my whole heart.
Make your Word come alive to me.
Thank you that I get to
read your Word and
it still speaks to me.

April 23

Guard Your Heart

Guard your heart above all else,
for it determines the course of your life.
~ Proverbs 4:23

Before I had a personal relationship with Jesus, negative, self-critical thoughts clouded my mind. I felt burdened by my own sense of unworthiness and guilt. It was then that I realized I needed to give those thoughts to my Savior. Jesus Christ is the CEO of heaven and earth, the one with the ultimate say over everything—especially our thoughts. Even when I felt too flawed to be forgiven, my King's voice broke through, offering a different perspective. Once I made the conscious decision to submit my thoughts to God and his authority, those guilty whispers lost their power.

Jesus always guarded his heart. If the Son of God needed to, shouldn't we strive to do the same? God tells us to guard our hearts above all else. But how can we accomplish this? We can be transformed if we make one decision: "I will submit my thoughts to the authority of Jesus." The Bible reminds us that only the Lord gives wisdom to use as a shield to protect the innocent (Proverbs 2:6–11).

What thoughts do you need to submit to Jesus's authority? Remember, when you give him control, the lies and accusations that hold you down have no room to stay. Through generations, wisdom and understanding from God have proven their power, guiding us away from evil and toward a life rooted in his truth.

Heavenly Father, guard my heart,
direct my path,
and keep me close to you.
Grant me the strength
to submit every thought
to your authority,
knowing that your wisdom protects me.

April 24
A Heavenly Address

There is more than enough room in my Father's home.
If this were not so,
would I have told you that
I am going to prepare a place for you?
~ John 14:2

Whenever my husband and I set out on a short road trip, I relish the excitement of exploring somewhere new. But no matter how enjoyable the journey is, I always find myself eager to return home—a familiar ranch nestled just ten miles outside a small town. It's my place of comfort and belonging.

When Jesus told his disciples that he was going to prepare a place for them, he also assured us that when we die, we are heading to a precise, prepared location—a heavenly address. We do not simply vanish or cease to exist. Jesus's promise was clear: "In my Father's house are many mansions" (John 14:2 KJV). For those who trust in

Jesus as their Savior, a place is waiting—an incredible estate in heaven.

As believers, we hold fast to the hope that death is not an end but a transition to eternal life in our heavenly home. We are not lost; in fact, we are more alive than ever before. Jesus spoke these words to comfort his disciples, who were troubled by the thought of his departure. He promised them that they need not fear death, for he was preparing a place for them. And with that assurance, he spoke of the Holy Spirit, who would come to guide and comfort them. May we, too, find peace in this promise.

Lord, we seek your guidance and
the reassurance of your promise
as we walk this life.
Help us to hold fast to the truth
that you have prepared a place for us,
so that our worries
may be lightened and
our hearts lifted.

April 25
No Surprise Endings

You are my refuge and my shield;
your word is my source of hope.
~ Psalm 119:114

As a little girl, I remember eagerly asking my mother to play hide-and-seek with me on rainy days. I knew all the best hiding spots in our home. Hearing her call, "Ready or not, here I come," would set my heart racing in the dark closet where I hid. The space seemed smaller and darker with each second as I waited for her to find me.

Psalm 119:105 (NASB) tells us, "Your word is a lamp to my feet and a light to my path." Just as I longed for the light in that gloomy closet, God's Word is the light that keeps us from stumbling through life. He loves us too much to leave us in the dark, and his truth remains true for today and all of time. With God, there are no surprise endings; his faithfulness endures.

The hope found in Scripture is indescribable. Thankfully, the

Word of God is unchanging and steadfast. Jesus said, "I tell you the truth, until heaven and earth disappear, not the smallest letter, not the least stroke of a pen, will by any means disappear from the Law" (Matthew 5:18). This assurance means that God's promises hold true forever.

Our God is not a rigid or unfeeling ruler. He is a loving Father who guides us because he knows what is best. He is aware of the challenges and pitfalls we face, and out of his great love for us, he directs us along the right path.

Heavenly Father, thank you for being our refuge
and source of light.
Help us to trust in your unchanging word
and to seek your guidance
in every step we take.
Remind us that your love and promises
are constant, giving us the assurance
we need to face whatever
comes our way.

April 26
A Visit with God

Trust in the LORD with all your heart;
do not depend on your own understanding.
Seek his will in all you do,
and he will show you which path to take.
~ Proverbs 3:5–6

Jesus, I've realized that when I stay tuned in to you, your guidance touches every part of my day. Whether it's the simple chores, like housework or emptying the dishwasher (which I really dislike), or moments when I pick up the phone to offer comfort to a friend grieving the loss of a loved one, your presence makes all the difference.

It's taken years, through many trials and moments of learning, for God to bring me to an understanding of the importance of seeking my Savior's will. The key is simple yet profound: surrender. I think of all the times I stubbornly pushed on doors of opportunity, trying to force them open, only to be met with silence. And then there were those moments that with the slightest touch, the path unfolded before me. In those moments, happiness, unexpected opportunities, spiritual gifts, and deeper friendships rained down like blessings from above.

Today, life calls once again. This day, I begin anew, striving to rely on you completely, knowing that your wisdom reaches far beyond my understanding. Your presence has taught me that it's not just in the small, daily actions that I need you, but also in the major turning points and the deep valleys of my life.

Lord, help me to lean on you
with all my heart and trust in your wisdom.
Guide my steps and help me to seek your will in all I do.
May I recognize that your plan for me is perfect,
even when I don't see the full picture.
Grant me the patience and faith to follow your lead,
and let your presence bring peace
in every moment.

April 27
Someone Other Than Me at the Controls

Creation looks forward to the day
when it will join God's children
in glorious freedom from death and decay.
~ Romans 8:21

The other day, I sat at my computer, mindlessly sorting through emails—deleting junk mail, fashion ads, and political flyers—when one unmarked email caught my eye. Without a second thought, I clicked on it. Almost immediately, I realized my mistake: my computer had been hacked. An unseen intruder had taken over, controlling my device and navigating every click. I felt vulnerable and unsettled, as though my personal space had been invaded.

After a frantic call to my bank and taking steps to secure my accounts, I breathed a sigh of relief, grateful the situation had been contained. But the incident made me think about a more insidious virus: sin. Just as that email disguised itself as legitimate, sin often appears harmless at first glance. God created our first parents, Adam and Eve, perfect and unblemished, providing for their every need and blessing them with a relationship of pure intimacy with their Creator. But temptation whispered, and they rebelled, refusing to accept God's direction. Does that sound familiar? It was at that precise moment that humanity was infected with the virus of sin.

Deep down, we know that this world is not as it should be, and neither are we. We wrestle with the conflict between the desires of the flesh and the deeper longings of the soul. But there is hope: a day will come when all will be restored—not because we are in control or manage to navigate perfectly, but because our Creator is.

God, I recognize that I am not in control
and never will be.
Thank you for the promise that one day
all will be made new.
Help me to surrender my struggles
with sin and seek your grace at the cross.
Guide me in trusting you,
not only in times of trouble
but in every moment.

April 28
God Sees Us Even Through Dense Fog

How great is our LORD!
His power is absolute!
His understanding is beyond comprehension!
~ Psalm 147:5

If you've ever driven at night in dense fog, you know the unnerving feeling of losing your sense of direction. That's exactly what happened to me a few nights ago. The road leading to my home, so familiar in daylight, became a disorienting path where I struggled to see even the center stripe. Turning on the high beams only made things worse, scattering the light and obscuring the way even more. For a moment I felt like a lost child, unsure whether I had missed the turn or passed my county road marker.

In many ways, this experience mirrors how God, in his omniscience, watches over us. He sees everything—where we are, where we're heading, and the next move we're about to make. Even when we drift across life's "center stripe," he knows and shouts his warnings, though we don't always hear or heed them.

I often reflect on the moments when I was too busy, stubborn, or preoccupied to listen to his quiet voice of caution. Those moments remind me that while I may not always know the way or recognize the signs, God's understanding is infinite, and he sees the whole picture. He knows what is best for us, even when we don't. He knows what will bring us joy and what could lead us to harm. The key is trusting that his way is better than our own.

Heavenly Father, I praise you for your great power,
wisdom, and unending love.
Thank you for watching over me,
even when I am lost in the fog of my own making.
Help me to listen to your guidance,
trust your direction, and follow your path,
knowing that you see and know all.

April 29
Train Up a Child

Direct your children onto the right path,
and when they are older,
they will not leave it.
~ Proverbs 22:6

I can still recall the many private conversations my daddy and I shared when I was growing up. Most of them happened in the cab of his pickup truck as we drove to the ranch to check on the livestock's water supply. Those drives were special, moments carved out of our busy days when he shared wisdom that would shape my life.

One conversation in particular stands out. We discussed my work ethic and the jobs I would take during and after college. Before the conversation ended, he turned to me and said, "The hardest job you'll ever have is being a parent." At the time, I assumed he meant I shouldn't rush into marriage. Now, looking back, I know my daddy understood exactly what he was preparing me for.

Children don't need perfect parents; they need mothers and fathers who point them to a perfect Savior and guide them, even when it means setting boundaries and saying no. When a child reaches the threshold of adolescence, it's not the time to suddenly try instilling values or faith. By then, they are already a reflection of what they have seen and absorbed in their home.

Our children pick up on our habits, words, and values. They are watching, even when we don't realize it. To give them a good start is not about achieving perfection but honoring God through our example and the legacy we leave.

Heavenly Father, help me to be the parent
and mentor who leads by example,
pointing the children in my life to you.
Give me the patience, wisdom, and strength
to nurture them in a way that reflects your love and truth.
May my efforts bring honor to your name
and guide them on a path that
they will not depart from.

April 30
Are You Available?

"Rabbi," his disciples asked him,
"why was this man born blind?
Was it because of his own sins or his parents' sins?"
"It was not because of his sins or his parents' sins,"
Jesus answered. "This happened so the power of God
could be seen in him."
~ John 9:2–3

The apostles had seen that familiar expression on Jesus's face before—that intense, determined look right before he performed another miracle. They watched as their Rabbi worked his mouth, rotating his jaw, gathering enough saliva. There might have been an audible "Yuck!" or perhaps a gasp that slipped out from the crowd when he spit onto the ground. Then he made a mud mixture with his fingers and gently spread it across the blind man's eyes. To the onlookers, it must have seemed odd, even unsettling, but what followed was astounding. The man became jubilant as his sight was restored. And yet, despite the miracle, the Pharisees refused to believe.

Once again, the simple became sacred. The ordinary was transformed into the extraordinary. God has a history of using the mundane—stones, sticks, spit—to accomplish his will. It makes me realize, *If God can use such simple things, why wouldn't he use you or me?*

Being available is the key. Jesus's mission and miracles are often missed by those who consider themselves "wise" by worldly standards. It's not about credentials or titles; it's about the willingness to be used by him, even when the task is unexpected or unglamorous.

Lord, help me to be available for your purposes,
no matter how small or simple the task may seem.
Remind me that your power is made perfect
in the ordinary moments of life.
Use me as an instrument of your will
so that your glory can be seen
through my willingness to serve.

May

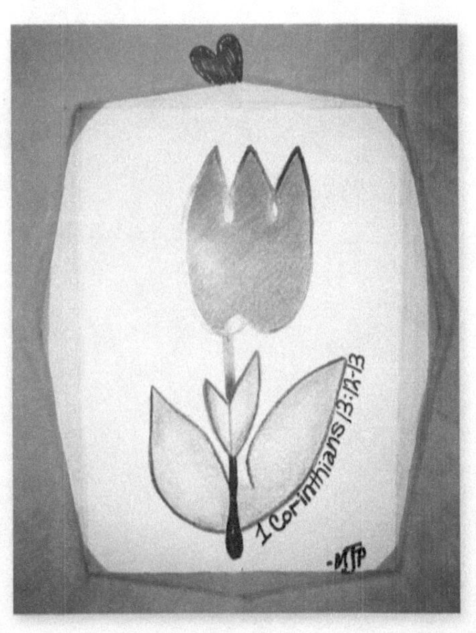

May 1
Are You "Hit and Miss" or Intentional?

Remember this—a farmer who plants
only a few seeds
will get a small crop.
But the one who plants generously
will get a generous crop.
~ 2 Corinthians 9:6

Being intentional in our Christian walk means actively choosing to experience the fullness of God in every aspect of our life. It requires determination and an unwillingness to settle for anything less than God's best. The blessings we receive are often in direct proportion to how we respond to his invitations.

This truth carries transformative potential. When we invest wholeheartedly in our relationship with God—through prayer, worship, and immersing ourselves in his Word—we unlock the full dimensions of what it means to be children of God. But this doesn't come without effort. Staying faithful in prayer, even when words don't come easily, and participating fully in worship, even on days when it feels routine, are key steps.

I recall a time when my prayers felt dry and worship seemed hollow; it felt like I was experiencing a "hit and miss" relationship with God. It was then that I decided to sow with intentionality. I set aside distractions and approached my spiritual life with renewed purpose. Over time, what started as small steps of faith blossomed into a deeper connection to my Creator.

Our Christian growth is directly influenced by the seeds we sow. If we are halfhearted, we can only expect a limited return. But if we give generously of our time, love, and commitment, we can look forward to an abundant spiritual harvest.

Heavenly Father, help me to live intentionally and
sow generously in my walk with you.
Strengthen my commitment to stay in your Word,
pray faithfully, and worship wholeheartedly.
May my efforts bear fruit that glorifies and
enriches my relationship with you.

May 2

Looking Good on the Outside—
What Does the Inside Look Like?

In their greed they will make up
clever lies to get hold of your money.
But God condemned them long ago,
and their destruction will not be delayed.
~ 2 Peter 2:3

Jesus cautioned the people of his time to be wary of leaders who, though impressive on the outside, were deceitful and corrupt at heart. These individuals knew how to use their charisma and influence to manipulate others for personal gain. The same is true today: appearances can be deceiving. A great preacher is not always a great Christian. The same holds true for a great scientist winning a Pulitzer Prize, or a marvelous actor winning an Oscar.

What, then, does a Spirit-filled person look like? They reflect Christ. Their lives are marked by love, joy, peace, patience, and other fruit of the Spirit that stand out in a world often filled with greed and turmoil. Christ himself was no passive figure. He stood up to critics, showing courage and wisdom in the face of opposition. He engaged with the intellectuals of his day and spoke the truth boldly.

As followers of Christ, we are not called to blend in to the background but to stand out as examples of God's transformative power. Christ was neither pretentious nor intimidating, and we should strive to be the same, embodying authenticity and strength in a humble manner.

Dear Jesus Christ, help me to actively listen to the truth
found in your Word and compare everything in the world
to your standard, especially when the messages sound so appealing.
May I strive to embody your character, inside and out,
and reflect your truth in everything I do.

May 3
Don't Ignore the Warnings!

The Lord says, "I will give you back what you lost
to the swarming locusts, the hopping locusts,
the stripping locusts, and the cutting locusts.
It was I who sent this great destroying army against you."
~ Joel 2:25

I had watched that yellow light blink on my dashboard for weeks. When I finally brought my car in for inspection, they told me the irritating little glow was only a computer glitch. *No big deal*, I thought. But caution indicators in life, just like the warning light on my dash, are not to be taken lightly.

Warnings come in all shapes and forms, signaling that something is amiss. Red lights in life signal impending danger. Sirens sound when a marriage is struggling, alarms ring when faith starts to falter, and flares go up when morals begin to erode. These warnings may show up as guilt, feelings of depression, or the tendency to rationalize poor choices. They may appear through a concerned friend's words or the sting of a convicting Scripture. No matter the form, their purpose is the same: to alert and wake us up.

Lord, help me to recognize the warnings you place in my life
and give me the wisdom to respond to them.
Open my heart to hear your voice
when you seek to get my attention.
May I recognize your signs
so that I can turn back to you
and walk in your ways.

May 4
Surround Me with Your Victory Song

For you are my hiding place;
you protect me from trouble.
You surround me with songs of victory.
~ Psalm 32:7

It's been said that when faith is strong, troubles become trifles. This doesn't mean that our challenges aren't real or that we should pretend they don't exist.

When I experience betrayal, my first response isn't pretty. My heart screams in anger and retribution. Walking through those tough times forces me to focus on God in faith and trust him despite the circumstances. Even in our darkest moments, he has never abandoned us and holds plans for our future. Only through Christ can we even find an optimistic spirit when all seems lost.

God knows the weight of our burdens and takes them seriously—so seriously that he sent his Son, Jesus Christ, to address the root cause: sin. Just as Christ overcame death, so our heavenly Father helps us rise above the troubles we face.

Have you ever watched someone endure unimaginable loss and yet, over time, learn to smile again? Or have you yourself experienced a hardship you thought would break you, only to find strength and healing as the days passed? It's a testament to God's power to bring beauty from ashes and turn pain into songs of victory.

Mercifully, God delivers those who *persevere* in the faith.

Lord, be my hiding place and
surround me with your songs of victory.
Remind me that through every trial and trouble,
you are present, guiding me to triumph through faith.
Strengthen my spirit
so I may see your hand at work and find hope,
even when life feels overwhelming.

May 5

An Animalistic Response

But to you who are willing to listen,
I say, love your enemies!
Do good to those who hate you.
Bless those who curse you.
Pray for those who hurt you.
~ Luke 6:27–28

It's easy to love those who love us back. But when we face mistreatment, our initial, primal response is often to fight back, to seek retaliation and retribution. We instinctively clench our fists and plot how to even the score.

While getting even may seem justified, it is not spiritual. God reminds us that vengeance is not our job—it is his. Judgment and justice are his responsibilities. He has never asked us to settle the score, not even once.

When we attempt to take matters into our own hands, it's as if we're declaring, "God can't handle it!"

In God's kingdom, however, the rule is grace. If we were to examine the soul of the vengeful, we would find the tumor of bitterness growing within, a spiritual carcinoma that darkens the heart. While we cannot change the past or undo the pain inflicted on us, we do have control over how we respond to it. Forgiveness is not about declaring that the one who wronged us was right. It is an acknowledgment that God is just and will handle everything in his perfect time. For Christians, forgiving those who sin against us is a privilege only available to those who have already been forgiven of so much.

Dear Father in heaven, guide me in following your divine example.
Help me to let go of my desire for revenge
and to trust that you will do what is right.
Teach me to respond with grace, love, and forgiveness,
knowing that your justice and
wisdom are perfect.

May 6
The Casual Christian

For they keep talking about the wonderful welcome
you gave us and how you turned away
from idols to serve the living and true God.
~ 1 Thessalonians 1:9

I've come to realize that the casual Christian has little to no influence on others. It took me time to learn this, but I've found that the Christian who refuses to compromise on honesty, integrity, and morality makes an effective witness for Christ. The worldly Christian—one who goes along with what the world does and excuses dishonest or unethical behavior—loses the courage to stand apart for fear of disapproval. I know this because that was me not so long ago.

Living a life that bears witness to Christ requires daily obedience to the voice of the Holy Ghost. We are called to die to self and maintain constant fellowship with God. Only then can we live in a way that reflects his presence and positively impacts this world, which is so often at odds with godly values.

I am still a work in progress. But with you as my witness, I no longer wish to be a "casual" Christian. My desire is to live a life marked by unwavering faith, not one that blends comfortably into the background.

Our Prince of Peace, I dedicate my life to you.
Teach me to speak with empathy,
to give with generosity, and to treat others with kindness.
Help me never to be a "casual" Christian.
Let there be nothing superficial about my devotion.
May I live boldly and sincerely for your glory.

May 7
Don't Let This Be a Wasted Season

The Lord himself watches over you!
The Lord stands beside you
as your protective shade.
~ Psalm 121:5

For a tree or any plant to grow and bear fruit, its seed must first be planted in the ground and die. In the same way, for spiritual fruit to emerge in our lives, we must be rooted in the Word of God and learn to die to self. It is through times of chastening, adversity, discipline, and affliction that God's Word nourishes us, allowing fruit to appear. This transformation does not happen overnight; it requires time and patience.

We've all experienced moments when, even after doing our best, we find ourselves waiting—whether it's for a teacher's approval, a boss's decision, or an answer to prayer. It is in these moments of waiting that God's promise holds true. He may seem slow to arrive, but he is never too late.

May 7

Are you in a season of waiting? Don't let it be a wasted one. Use this time to draw closer to God in prayer, so that when he speaks, you'll recognize his voice and be ready to move. Waiting is not passive; it's an opportunity to grow and prepare for what's ahead.

Almighty God, help me trust in your timing,
even when I can't see the full picture.
Let me use this season of waiting to draw closer to you,
confident that you are working in my heart
and the hearts of others to bring about your plan.
Teach me patience, strengthen my faith,
and guide me in your ways.

May 8
The Clouds of Life

The Lord went ahead of them.
He guided them during the day with a pillar of cloud,
and he provided light at night with a pillar of fire.
This allowed them to travel by day or by night.
~ Exodus 13:21

The children of Israel had a profound reminder of God's presence: a pillar of cloud by day and a pillar of fire by night. They only moved when the cloud moved, trusting completely in God's guidance.

Clouds will come into our lives, too. If you haven't taken the time to gaze at the evening sky recently, let me encourage you to sit quietly and soak in the beauty of God's creation. Each sunset is an artistic masterpiece painted by his hand. While clouds can sometimes bring storms, they can also reveal the glory of God. Through them, he speaks, reminding us of his presence and purpose. As the Bible says,

"The LORD went before them by day in a pillar of cloud to lead the way" (Exodus 13:21).

Perhaps you find yourself in a wilderness today—a wilderness of a broken relationship, financial trouble, disappointment, doubt, or sin that you cannot let go. Just as he did for the Israelites, God goes before you to encourage and guide you. He is with you, even in the clouds of life. Look up, and you'll see his presence.

God can see what we cannot. He knows our needs and the hazards along the path, and he will protect and provide for us. Trust in God, even when the clouds seem dark and heavy.

Lord, thank you for your constant presence,
even in the storms and clouds of life.
Help me to trust in your guidance
and remember that you see what I cannot.
Lead me through my wilderness,
and teach me to look up and
recognize your glory.

May 9
Odd Man Out

But they were looking for a better place,
a heavenly homeland.
That is why God is not ashamed to be called their God,
for he has prepared a city for them.
~ Hebrews 11:16

We live in an upside-down world. People hate when they should love, quarrel when they should be friendly, fight when they should seek peace, and choose wrong when they should do right.

There's a story about a toy clown with a weight in its head. No matter how it was positioned—on its feet or its side—it always flipped upside down. This imagery brings to mind the disciples, and in many ways, it reflects our own lives. To the world, the disciples seemed like misfits, oddities who didn't conform. I know when I'm around a large group of unbelievers, I don't feel like I fit in, like I'm the odd man out.

I'm sure for non-believers, a true Christian can seem like an abnormality.

All around us, people who don't have the peace that comes only from God sense that something is wrong with their topsy-turvy lives. They yearn for stability, for a way to be set right side up. Only our Creator has the power to transform and reorient a person, placing them firmly on their feet.

Lord, help us to be heroes of the faith,
even in our imperfections.
Teach us to trust you completely
and to dedicate our lives to you,
knowing that only you
can make what is upside down
right again.

May 10
God Wants Your Undivided Attention

Come close to God,
and God will come close to you.
Wash your hands, you sinners;
purify your hearts,
for your loyalty is divided between God and the world.
~ James 4:8

What a remarkable promise this verse holds. Each of us is invited to draw near to God, with the assurance that he will draw near to us. This is the greatest experience we can have, yet for most of us, it doesn't come easily.

Life is full of distractions. Children, work, television, the internet, and even church activities can consume our time, leaving little space to be alone with God. When I finally confessed that God was in charge and I was not, a weight lifted from my shoulders. I no longer needed to figure out life on my own. The relief was immense, but it required me to surrender my divided loyalties.

Perhaps it's time to readjust our priorities. Maybe we need to say no to certain activities or demands on our time. Whatever it takes, make space to be with God. As God's Word promises, "Come near to God and he will come near to you" (James 4:8 NIV). God is always ready to meet with you and is glad when you come to him.

Lord, help me to remove distractions and
make you my priority. Teach me
to set aside time to be with you,
knowing that true service begins
as you humble my heart and
draw me closer to you.

May 11
Where Is God in Times of Trouble?

Give your burdens to the LORD,
and he will take care of you.
He will not permit the godly to slip and fall.
~ Psalm 55:22

Years ago, I came across the oft-quoted prayer by Protestant theologian Reinhold Niebuhr: "God grant me the serenity to accept things I cannot change, the courage to change the things I can, and wisdom to know the difference."[1] This prayer captures a vital truth: of how one should always *pray*—and then *live*.

When my daughter Carmen was diagnosed with cystic fibrosis as a baby, the doctors explained that it was irreversible—a condition she would live with all her life. At first, I rejected their words, holding tightly to my faith in God's power to heal. I knew my Lord could remove that disease if he chose. Over time, however, we realized that God was going to heal Carmen on the other side of eternity, as she lived as a child and then as an adult with this physical challenge. Our family had to adapt.

There are some things in life that God calls us to accept. Stressing about what we cannot change only drains our energy and steals our peace. As someone once said, "Worry is the interest paid on trouble before it comes due." Instead, God taught our family to lean on and trust in him.

Is there a situation in your life that you've been fighting to change, but God may be calling you to trust him? Lay that burden at his feet and trust him to guide you through it.

Lord, help me to surrender the burdens
I cannot change and trust in your wisdom and care.
Teach me to rely on your strength
in all circumstances and find peace
in your unchanging presence.

May 12

Do You Allow Your
Thoughts to Run Your Life?

We destroy every proud obstacle
that keeps people from knowing God.
We capture their rebellious thoughts and
teach them to obey Christ.
~ 2 Corinthians 10:5

How often do we speak as if we are powerless over our thoughts? We might say, "Don't talk to me, I'm in a bad mood," as if our feelings are a place where we are forced to reside. Or we warn others, "Don't mess with him; he has a terrible disposition," as though the human disposition is a permanent, unchangeable state. Are we merely victims of the emotional "bacteria" of the moment?

The truth is, we are not helpless. Our assignment is clear: to guard our minds and refuse entry to harmful thoughts. When trashy or rebellious thoughts surface, we must act immediately and declare, "This heart belongs to God! Selfishness, envy, bitterness—you are not welcome here!" By taking such a stand, we align our minds with Christ.

What if we made it our daily goal to capture every thought, good or bad, and submit it to God? What if we resolved to let no rubbish settle in our minds? God reminds us, "Be very careful about what you think. Your thoughts run your life" (Proverbs 4:23 ICB). When we guard our minds, we gain the clarity and strength to live with purpose and love.

*Abba Father, teach me to take every thought captive
and make it obedient to Christ. Build me into a leader
who guards my mind and heart,
that I may go into the world
and ignite it with your love.*

May 13

Do You Allow Your
Thoughts to Run Your Life?

May the LORD continually bless you from Zion.
May you see Jerusalem prosper as long as you live.
May you live to enjoy your grandchildren.
May Israel have peace!
~ Psalm 128:5–6

Family life often feels like a string of crisis situations. The little ones who once cooed and gurgled grow into independent adolescents with their own ideas and challenges. The protective environment of home is disrupted by school, new friends, financial strain, illnesses, accidents, and the endless demands of a busy schedule. Most of us have faced at least one, if not all, of these surmountable problems at the same time.

Now, let's throw in dating, new drivers, and kids leaving for college and moving out! If that doesn't complete the picture of a chaotic family life, I'm not sure what will. It can feel overwhelming, but what does God say about these years? He says we are blessed. He says we will be happy. And he promises that it will "be well" with us if we place God at the center of our families.

Is God the head of your family? That is the foundation for his blessings. My mother often reminded me, "This too shall pass, my dear." She was wise, and she was right. Those trying years eventually give way to a new season, and I now find myself enjoying my grandchildren, marveling at how God has guided us through.

> *Everlasting Father, help me make you the head*
> *of my home. Teach me to pray for my family daily,*
> *trusting that with you at the center,*
> *I will find blessing, happiness,*
> *and peace.*

May 14

Holy Spirit–Teacher and Guide

When the Spirit of truth comes,
he will guide you into all truth.
He will not speak on his own
but will tell you what he has heard.
He will tell you about the future.
~ John 16:13

My husband and I usually know where we are going when we jump in the car. This particular time, we were on our way to a new location. Frustrated and lost for too long, we finally pulled out our GPS, which guided us right to our destination. We laughed at our foolishness and asked ourselves, "Why didn't we use that earlier?"

Too many times, we rely on our own strength and not the Holy Spirit. When we receive Jesus Christ as our Savior and Lord, the Holy Spirit takes up residence in our heart. At that very instant, he begins to dwell within us. The Bible says, "If anyone does not have the Spirit of Christ, they do not belong to Christ" (Romans 8:9 NIV).

The presence of the Holy Spirit is the defining mark of belonging to God and becoming a Christian.

The Holy Spirit helps us with life's struggles in four ways. First, he convicts us of sin, gently but firmly leading us to repentance and a closer walk with God. Second, he is our teacher, instructing us as we meditate on God's Word and guiding us into deeper understanding and truth. Third, he intercedes for us, morphing our prayers into agreement with God's will. And last, he bears our burdens, advocates for us, and gives us courage. The Holy Spirit is our trusted guide. He not only provides wisdom but also offers the assurance that we are never alone on our journey.

Holy Spirit, teach me to listen for your voice
and follow your guidance throughout each day.
You are my GPS for life, and I trust you
to lead me in truth and righteousness.

May 15

It's Your Choice

As ranchers, we have experienced seasons of drought over the years. Those seasons make it hard to trust God when he seems to withhold the much-needed rain. This verse in the Psalms reminds us of God's faithfulness in restoring his people after decades of hardship. If God could bring restoration to Israel then, why wouldn't he continue to do so for us today? His promises endure, and his faithfulness is unchanging, since God is immutable and without time.

God's Word encourages us to meditate on the promises found in it continually. When the Lord commissioned Joshua, God told his brave new leader to keep the truths found in Scripture "always on your lips; meditate on it day and night, so that you may be careful to do everything written in it. Then you will be prosperous and successful" (Joshua 1:8 NIV).

True success isn't about personal power or networking with the "right people," as the world teaches. Instead, it's about aligning our lives with God's Word and trusting in God.

So, who are your "right people?" For me, it's simple: just give me Jesus. He is the only one who brings restoration, purpose, and true prosperity.

Lord, thank you for your faithfulness
in restoring your people during times of difficulty.
Teach me to meditate on your Word
and trust in your promises.
May I choose you above all else,
knowing that you are the source of
true success and restoration.

May 16
Beware of the Danger Zone!

Just think how much more the blood of Christ will purify our consciences from sinful deeds so that we can worship the living God. For by the power of the eternal Spirit, Christ offered himself to God as a perfect sacrifice for our sins.

~ Hebrews 9:14

Is the Holy Spirit tugging at your heart about something that isn't right in your life? Are you engaging in something you know dishonors Jesus? Are you walking in a manner that glorifies God? Would other people identify you as a follower of Christ through your words and actions? These are tough questions, but they are essential for spiritual growth.

The Bible teaches that the human conscience is defiled by sin, making it an unreliable guide when left to its own devices. Without the purifying work of the Holy Spirit, our consciences can be twisted by Satan to convince us that wrong is right. This is why yielding our hearts and minds to Christ is so important. Only then can our conscience serve as a faithful warning system.

God often uses our conscience to alert us when we are entering dangerous territory. Don't ignore that inner voice or dismiss it as unimportant. Instead, face your sin, confess it, and take steps to make it right. When we allow Christ to cleanse our heart, we can worship the living God with freedom and peace.

Thank you, God, for the gift of a conscience
that warns me when I'm straying into dangerous territory.
Help me to heed your voice and
surrender my heart to the purifying work of your Spirit.
I pray for your peace to surround me and
for the courage to make things right.

May 17
Follow Me

Your word is a lamp to guide my feet
and a light for my path.
~ Psalm 119:105

I marvel at my four-legged companion, Dude, who attentively waits for my command to "sit," "come here," "give me your paw," and "give me a kiss." His obedience isn't hesitant or questioning; it's immediate and heartfelt. He intimately knows and obeys his master, which is me.

As Christians, we have only one authority, one compass: the Word of God. Throughout our day, there are thousands of different voices, all claiming their own authority and clamoring for our allegiance, but there is only one voice that will tell us the truth. That voice is from the written Word of God, given to us by the Lord to tell us what we are to believe and how we are to live.

What are you using to guide your path today? Some follow public opinion or what feels good at the moment. Jesus simply says, "Follow me." Sounds easy, but so many of us struggle with that simple command.

Yet, even with such a direct invitation, we often wrestle with surrendering control.

If I could be as obedient to my Lord as Dude is to me!

Creator of the universe, may this testimony,
exalted by your Word made flesh,
be a daily reminder of the complete and
perfect standard of truth, reality,
and behavior.

May 18
Living in Obedience to the Lord

Try to please them all the time,
not just when they are watching you.
As slaves of Christ, do the will of God
with all your heart.
~ Ephesians 6:6

Here's a simple question: If you truly love someone, would you intentionally hurt them? Would you go out of your way to make them feel unloved or punished just because they didn't meet your expectations? Of course not. Genuine love seeks to build up, not tear down.

I would never intentionally hurt the ones I love. Actually, it's the opposite. I try to do everything I can to bless them!

God's love for us as his children operates on an even higher plane. Because of our Father's deep and abiding love, he doesn't leave us to wander aimlessly through life. He cares too much to allow us to live without direction or purpose. His will for us is not restrictive but redemptive, designed to bring meaning and fulfillment to our lives.

Coveting God's will for our life isn't about obligation; it's about trust. A Christian cannot find true peace or contentment outside of God's will because we were created to live in harmony with our Creator's plan. His will is where we discover joy, clarity, and purpose.

Loving Father, help us to honor your will for our lives
and to love our neighbors as ourselves.
Teach us to walk in obedience, not out of fear,
but out of a desire to live fully
in the abundance of your love.

May 19
Saul, Meet the Savior

So Ananias went and found Saul.
He laid his hands on him and said,
"Brother Saul, the Lord Jesus,
who appeared to you on the road,
has sent me so that you
might regain your sight and
be filled with the Holy Spirit."
~ Acts 9:17

Like Saul who was renamed Paul, many of us have faced moments of crushing solitude—alone with the weight of our sins and the brokenness of our choices. I know I have. My past (especially my teenage years) is littered with poor choices covered by the blood of Christ. During those moments, when God drops the scales from our eyes, and we can see the weight and cost of our sins, we might feel like it's too late for grace. But the truth in Scripture reminds us that it's never too late.

This verse carries a powerful message. If you show someone their failures without introducing them to Jesus, the weight of guilt can leave them hopeless. Offer someone religion without revealing the depths of their sin, and pride may blind them to their need for grace. But bring sin and the Savior together in the same heart, and something miraculous happens. Grace transforms guilt, and redemption turns broken lives into testimonies of God's power.

Paul's story is proof that no one is beyond God's reach. A persecutor became a preacher; an enemy of the faith became its greatest champion. Stranger things have indeed happened.

Forgiving Father, help me to see those who oppose my faith
not as enemies, but as people in need of your transformative love.
May I be faithful in extending the same grace
I've received.

May 20
A Reflection of Christ

Thank you for making me
so wonderfully complex!
Your workmanship is marvelous—
how well I know it.
~ Psalm 139:14

Yesterday, I was reminded of one of the most cherished birthday gifts I've ever received: a homemade banana pudding. So often, on my special day, this extraordinary woman makes me my favorite dessert. I feel seen, heard, and loved.

It wasn't just the pudding that made it special, but the love and effort poured into it by a dear friend who, despite our rare interactions, took the time to make something just for me. Isn't that a reflection of God's presence in our lives?

We are more than just bodies with flesh and blood. What makes us extraordinary isn't our physical makeup but the Creator's signature imprint on us. We are designed in his image, uniquely crafted to do good deeds, to love, and to reflect his character. Our value doesn't come from what we accomplish but from whose we are. Thankfully, we are God's.

The friend I so lovingly speak of touches many lives daily, weekly, and monthly. Her kindness touches lives in ways that mirror the heart of Christ, reminding me that we are all called to reflect his love and grace to those around us.

Creator and Author of my life, thank you
for shaping me in your image and for giving me
a purpose rooted in your love.
May my life reflect your workmanship
and bring glory to you.
Help me always reflect
your presence in my life.

May 21
The Highest Calling

So you cannot become my disciple
without giving up everything you own.
~ Luke 14:33

One of my dear friends was offered a position with a prestigious company. It came with a significant pay increase, impressive perks, and the promise of a successful trajectory. Yet, the more she prayed over the decision, she couldn't shake a deep sense of unease. God was gently but firmly leading her in a different direction, one in the nonprofit arena. Turning down that offer felt counterintuitive at the time, but looking back, she saw how that decision provided hope to the multitudes and brought peace that no paycheck could ever provide.

God's calling is always noble, whether it leads you to parenthood, building a multi-million-dollar business, or serving in the mission field. The true measure of a person and a position's value isn't found in its paycheck but in whether what you are doing aligns with God's will for your life.

Most of us won't stand behind a pulpit or travel to distant lands as missionaries. Yet, every believer is called to follow Christ with unwavering faithfulness. We're called to reflect his presence wherever he places us—in the classroom, the home, the office, or the community. We're called to be Spirit-led, walking as God's ambassadors to bring his light into the world.

What is God calling you to do today? It may not look grand in the eyes of the world, but if it's his will, it is of eternal significance.

Lord God, may I dedicate my life
to fulfilling your will above all else.
Grant me the courage
to follow wherever you lead,
knowing that serving you
is the highest calling of all.

May 22

In Need of a New Heart?

But now is the time to get rid of anger, rage,
malicious behavior, slander, and dirty language.
Don't lie to each other,
for you have stripped off
your old sinful nature and
all its wicked deeds.
~ Colossians 3:8–9

Where did we get the idea that we can't change? I have heard others (and even myself) say things like, "It's in my genes; my grandfather had a temper," or "I've always been a pessimist; it's just who I am," or "I can't help worrying; it's part of my nature." Each of these statements is a denial of God's power in our lives.

I have often wondered if we would accept the same reasoning about our physical health. Can you imagine telling others, "It's just my nature to have a broken leg. I can't do anything about it!" Of course not. When our bodies are broken, we seek healing. Shouldn't we do the same with our attitudes and beliefs?

Jesus is in the heart transformation business. When we make those negative statements of unbelief, we are hamstringing God in our life. God can and does miracles even today! He offers us the free gift beyond comparison: a new heart fashioned after his own. Jesus's heart is

- pure—free from sin and selfishness;
- peaceful—resting in trust and obedience to our Father; and
- hope-filled—aligned with God's will in every way.

God's plan for you isn't a patched-up, slightly improved heart. His plan is to give you a new one filled with faith, molded in the likeness of his only Son. God can do anything!

Lord Jesus, transform my heart to reflect yours.
Fill me with faith as you change me.
May my relationship with you shine through
my words and actions,
drawing others to your love.

May 23
The Ultimate Prayer Partner

And the Holy Spirit helps us in our weakness.
For example, we don't know what
God wants us to pray for.
But the Holy Spirit prays for us
with groanings that cannot be expressed in words.
~ Romans 8:26

Have you ever faced a situation so overwhelming or confusing that you didn't even know how to pray? Or have you been so weighed down by grief or heartache that words seemed impossible to find? Most of us have been there, feeling lost and unable to articulate our hearts.

When words fail us, the Holy Spirit steps in, interceding for us with the desires of our hearts when we can't even begin to articulate them. He aligns our prayers with the perfect will of God, ensuring that even our deepest, unspoken needs are brought before the Father.

I've felt a divine partnership with God, unlike any other, during my darkest times. These are the moments of sweet comfort as the Holy Spirit brings the deepest, unspoken cries of our hearts before God's throne, interceding on our behalf. In those silent, wordless prayers, I have felt an overwhelming peace wash over me in my darkest hours. While I may be unable to explain it fully, I know with certainty where my help comes from. It's a comfort that words can't fully describe, but one I've come to treasure deeply.

God knows us better than anyone. He understands our hearts' cries, even when they remain unspoken. We must remember to turn to God in every situation, trusting that the Spirit is our ultimate prayer partner, faithfully carrying our needs to the throne of grace.

Lord God, thank you for the gift of the Holy Spirit,
who intercedes for me in my weakness.
Replace my fear with faith and fill me with the assurance that you hear
my every cry,
responding with love and mercy.
May I trust you more each day.

May 24

Freedom in Christ, Our Greatest Gift

Live wisely among those who are not believers,
and make the most of every opportunity.
~ Colossians 4:5

As Memorial Day approaches, I'm reminded of the men and women who do not know me by name yet paid the ultimate sacrifice with their lives so that I might enjoy the freedoms of this wonderful United States of America. Their selflessness inspires me to reflect on how I can use the freedom I've been given to share the greatest gift of all—Jesus Christ.

One of the most effective ways I've found to turn a conversation toward spiritual matters is to simply ask, "How can I pray for you?" Rarely do I receive a negative response. On the contrary, unbelievers are often deeply moved by this sincere expression of concern. It opens a door to share Christ's love in a personal and meaningful way.

Sharing the love of Christ doesn't happen if we wait passively for opportunities to arise. We must pray for boldness and actively seek ways to share our faith, especially with those we encounter regularly.

God knows us intimately. He knows our strengths and weaknesses. He is infinitely wise and good. He is never caught off guard, never panics, and never quits. When we surrender the controls of our lives to him, he charts our course with precision and care, and guides us safely through the storms of life.

Heavenly Father, thank you for the sacrifice
of those who have secured our freedoms.
Help me to use that freedom to share your love boldly.
Chart my course and guide my steps
from this day forward until eternity.
Teach me to trust you fully,
knowing you are always at the controls.

May 25
Simply Be Still

The Lord your God is with you,
the Mighty Warrior who saves.
He will take great delight in you;
in his love he will no longer rebuke you,
but will rejoice over you with singing.
~ Zephaniah 3:17 NIV

That verse got me today. I reread it again, swallowing hard on "The Lord your God is with you, the Mighty Warrior who saves." My heart is heavy, shattered for the parents whose children did not return home yesterday from Uvalde Elementary School. And yet, my mind is replaying the very Scripture I highlighted this morning at five a.m.: "The Lord your God is with you."

Deeply knowing the pain of these parents who have lost their children, I cried out to God to comfort them. I prayed they would be blessed with sweet assurances from our Lord and Savior.

There are moments during our walk when God simply wants us to be still and know that he is God (Psalm 46:10). Sometimes it is so hard to trust God during those dark moments as his angels sing over us. Does that feel impossible? Perhaps you might feel you're not worthy of such affection, love, or comfort. Neither was Judas, yet Jesus washed his feet. Neither was Peter, yet Jesus prepared breakfast for him. Neither are we, but Jesus died for us.

*Lord Jesus, help me to understand my grief and
to feel your presence in it.
Teach me to rest in your love,
knowing you sit with me in my sorrow,
blessing my grief even
as you have blessed my joys.*

May 26

Foggy Tragedies ... The
Suffering of the Broken Hearted

The faithful love of the LORD never ends!
His mercies never cease.
Great is his faithfulness;
his mercies begin afresh each morning.
I say to myself, "The LORD is my inheritance;
therefore, I will hope in him!"
~ Lamentations 3:22–24

Have you ever experienced the fog of the brokenhearted? I have. It descends suddenly and without mercy, imprisoning the soul in darkness. This heavy cloud doesn't honor schedules or respect status; it lingers, distorting our sense of direction and blurring the road ahead. Like when we are driving, we might try to spiritually dim our lights, slow our pace, and try to clear our vision, but nothing seems to help.

What brings this fog? It could be from the betrayal of a trusted friend, the heartbreak of a spouse walking away, or the sting of parental abandonment. It may come from standing beside a loved one's casket or keeping vigil by their sickbed. If you've faced these moments, you know the disorienting weight of this cloud.

Yet even in the midst of this haze, there is hope. Seeing God through the mist of pain transforms our suffering. In Jesus, God was never more human than in his Son's moments of agony on the cross. And it's through his pierced hands that we find our way out of the heaviness of the fog. The very hand that leads us out is one that intimately understands our pain.

Jeremiah, in his sorrow, found hope in God's unending love and mercy. His faithfulness renews us each morning, giving strength to endure and healing to persevere.

Faithful Lord, thank you for your steadfast love
that never fails, even in the fog.
Lead me through my dark hours
of suffering and renew me
with the hope that only
you can give.

May 27

Day of Remembrance

But those who trust in the LORD will find new strength.
They will soar high on wings like eagles.
They will run and not grow weary.
They will walk and not faint.
~ Isaiah 40:31

I remember visiting a cemetery as a child with my grandparents, placing flowers on the graves of family members. I didn't fully grasp the significance at the time, but now I understand. It wasn't just about loss; it was about honoring the lives they lived. Each name represented a story, a lesson, a love that still impacts the world today.

For many Americans, Memorial Day marks the "unofficial" beginning of summer with sweet barbecues and outdoor activities. More importantly, we get to honor the courageous men and women who gave their lives defending our country. Their sacrifice is the foundation of the liberties we enjoy today. This holiday is a day of remembrance, gratitude, and respect for those who paid the ultimate price.

While Memorial Day focuses on those who have passed, we also have an opportunity to express thanks to living service members. A simple "Thank you for your service" can go a long way in showing appreciation.

Also, let us be mindful of the families who have lost loved ones in service to our country. May we honor their sacrifices by fostering unity and living with gratitude for the freedoms their loved ones fought to protect.

Gracious Spirit, Creator of life,
make your presence known to me.
Help me to be brave in my remembering,
honest in my sorrow, and
open in my love and
compassion toward others.
May I honor the sacrifices of those who have
fallen by living a life of gratitude
and purpose.

May 28
God Controls the Clock

And now the prize awaits me—
the crown of righteousness,
which the Lord, the righteous Judge,
will give me on the day of his return.
And the prize is not just for me
but for all who eagerly look forward to his appearing.
~ 2 Timothy 4:8

Watching the news, I have often shaken my head and wondered, *Where is this world heading?* Since confusion and chaos seem to reign in the natural, it's easy to feel lost. Yet, those who stay rooted in God's Word know who controls the clock of destiny. Our King is always at work, quietly but powerfully moving to fulfill his unchanging plan and purpose.

Thankfully, God is not absent, no matter how things appear. By his providence, he sustains us, orchestrating all things to bring about his divine purpose. Paul described God's ultimate plan: "At the right time he will bring everything together under the authority of Christ—everything in heaven and on earth" (Ephesians 1:10). We are encouraged to rejoice, as one day Satan's rule will end and Christ will reign as Lord over all creation.

When the daily headlines sow fear and uncertainty, remember that God's people won't be surprised by the outcome. Our Father has already revealed how history will culminate—with the victory of his Son.

Let us eagerly await our Savior's return, living each day with faith and expectancy.

> *Dear Lord Jesus, guard me from deceit and*
> *lead me into truth and righteousness.*
> *May I eagerly look forward to your return,*
> *living with the assurance that your hand*
> *guides all things and*
> *your victory is certain.*

May 29
Flesh It Out

In view of all this,
make every effort to respond to God's promises.
Supplement your faith with a generous provision
of moral excellence, and moral excellence with knowledge.
~ 2 Peter 1:5

When I first became a Christian, I falsely thought that life would be easy. Now, I realize that being a follower of Christ isn't a passive calling. We are not to just believe and sit back to wait for eternity. Faith is our foundation, and God calls us to actively build on it. That's our part—making every effort to grow and respond to his promises.

Growth requires discipline; it's not some magical spell. It's about establishing "holy habits" and pacing ourselves for a lifelong journey of faith. Whether we look at a championship football team, a brilliant orchestra, or a thriving business, the common denominator is discipline. Likewise, our lives of faith need intentionality, order, and commitment.

Peter reminds us that the more we grow, "the more productive and useful [we] will be in [our] knowledge of our Lord Jesus Christ" (2 Peter 1:8). Growing in moral excellence, knowledge, and faith isn't just for our benefit; it equips us to serve God and others more effectively.

We must continue past belief and add to our faith by fleshing it out with action, discipline, and a heart dedicated to growth.

Lord God, strengthen my resolve
to work out your will in my life.
Help me to grow in faith,
knowledge, and service,
just as your faithful servants
have done before me.
May I honor you in all I do.

May 30
God Has Always Remained Faithful

Say to God,
"How awesome are your deeds!
Your enemies cringe before your mighty power."
~ Psalm 66:3

When I pray, I often picture God as a caring Father, not just a friend or a distant deity. My Abba intimately knows me as his child and treats me as part of his family with wisdom and love. It also enables me to trust him and his decisions explicitly, and this is no easy task—especially during difficult times. This perspective elevates how I approach him throughout my day—with awe, respect, and trust.

In today's world, many Christians focus their prayers on Jesus, and while that's wonderful, it's important to remember how Jesus taught us to pray—always to the Father. Thankfully, in Scripture, we also find the Holy Spirit interceding for us, even when we can't find the words to pray (Romans 8:26–27).

Waiting on God requires patience, but it also brings clarity. As we focus on his faithfulness, our vision clears and our hearts align with His will.

Let today be your "thank God" day! Look for blessings in the ordinary and the extraordinary—a beautiful tree, a radiant sunset, or even the challenges that shape our character, like a stubborn child, a gas-guzzling car, or a cranky neighbor or coworker. Gratitude, especially in the midst of trials, brings us closer to understanding God's faithfulness.

Father God, you are awesome and worthy of all praise.
Thank you for your guidance, provision,
and steadfast love. May my life
reflect my gratitude for all that
you are and all that you do.

May 31
Men Who Look Good on the Outside

He is especially hard on those
who follow their own twisted sexual desire,
and who despise authority.
These people are proud and arrogant,
daring even to scoff at supernatural beings
without so much as trembling.
~ 2 Peter 2:10

Another spiritual leader's fall into sexual temptation is blasted all over the media. Watching the intimate details of their sin play out in the news brings me to my knees in prayer, covering our pastors with a hedge of protection.

Jesus warned his followers to be vigilant against leaders who might appear righteous outwardly but are corrupt within. These are individuals who misuse their influence, leading others astray while satisfying their own selfish desires.

In contrast, Jesus offers the perfect picture of what a Spirit-filled life looks like. His life was defined by love, joy, peace, and patience, even in a broken and hostile world. He was not passive or weak; he confronted wrongs with authority and courage. Children adored him, sinners were drawn to him, and he spoke with a clarity that confounded his detractors.

At the end of his earthly life, Jesus faced the ultimate challenge—death itself—and emerged victorious. His life and resurrection remain the ultimate example of righteousness and power.

It's never too late to recalibrate our lives and follow our Savior's example. Let us guard our hearts and minds against those who would mislead us, and keep our eyes fixed on Christ, the true and perfect leader.

God in heaven, grant me discernment
to recognize false teachers and the wisdom
to follow only your truth.
Remind me to pray for our spiritual leaders.
Help me to live a life that reflects
the character of Christ,
the perfect example.

Want to Keep Going?

We hope you enjoyed your *Coffee with God: Joy in the Spring Mornings: 90 Sips of Strong Grace, Bold Faith, and Endless Mercy.*

Make sure you grab a copy of Debb Joy's next seasonal devotional, *Coffee with God: Joy in the Summer Mornings: 90 Sips of Strong Grace, Bold Faith, and Endless Mercy.*

And make sure you pick up Debb's *Coffee with God: Joy in the Autumn Mornings: 90 Sips of Strong Grace, Bold Faith, and Endless Mercy* as well as her
Coffee with God: Joy in the Winter Mornings: 90 Sips of Strong Grace, Bold Faith, and Endless Mercy.

About the Author

Debb Joy is a flower-loving, garden-digging, prayer-warrior Doodle with a heart full of grace and a shovel in hand. When life gets thorny, she heads to her garden—her sacred therapy spot—where planting flowers is her way of praying without words. She finds joy in the blooms, peace in the planting, and God's presence in the stillness.

Devotions are her daily fuel, and she treasures quiet moments spent in prayer, especially after a day with her grandsons or swapping laughs with her husband, Kerry, and her beloved daughter, Madolyn. Debb's family is her heartbeat and the reason her prayers are always full of gratitude.

Debb also has a secret addiction to that glorious endorphin high after a good workout, and to excellent coffee. And don't be fooled by the garden gloves; she's got running shoes too! Her comfort foods range from humble cottage cheese to soul-warming homemade potato soup. And when she wants a salad? You better believe it's loaded with grilled chicken and creamy avocado. But when stress calls? She answers with coffee and chocolate. She loves her coffee with lots of creamer and no sugar, and her chocolate coated in a candy shell—specifically plain M&M's, her tiny, colorful lifeline.

Through her writing, Debb shares faith, joy, and a little bit of chocolate-covered truth for the soul with whomever the Lord places in her path.

To have Debb Joy light up and speak at your upcoming event, email her at dpagejoy@gmail.com. She loves to share hope and the joy of Christ with her audience. Just make sure to provide plenty of M&M's and good coffee—not necessarily in that order!

About the Illustrator

Madolyn Phillips was practically born with a crayon in her hand. From her earliest days, creativity has been second nature, and though she isn't a professional graphic designer, she delights in anything that allows her to make art. Her illustrations shine throughout her mother's devotional series, *Coffee with God and Joy in the Mornings*, where her vibrant touch brings the words to life.

Madolyn refers to her Mom as her spiritual rock. Her husband, Chris, and two boys, Slade and Ryder, are her pride and joy. She finds comfort in spending time with her family. Going home to the ranch to see her parents is where she draws her strength as she enjoys God's portrait of the setting sun over West Texas skies.

Notes

March 22

1. "Jesus Christ is Risen Today," Hymnary, accessed May 6, 2024, https://hymnary.org/text/jesus_christ_is_risen_today_our_tri.

May 11

1. "The Serenity Prayer and Twelve Step Recovery," Hazelden Betty Ford Foundation, October 14, 2018,
https://www.hazeldenbettyford.org/articles/the-serenity-prayer#:~:text=There%20it%20was%20credited%20to,and%20other%20Twelve%20Step%20programs.